With My Last Breath

By Forrest L. Marion

That Others May Live: USAF Air Rescue In Korea (2004)

Brothers in Berets: The Evolution of Air Force Special Tactics, 1953-2003 (2018)

(With Jon T. Hoffman) *Forging a Total Force: The Evolution of the Guard and Reserve* (2018)

Flight Risk: The Coalition's Air Advisory Mission in Afghanistan, 2005-2015 (2018)

With My Last Breath

The Life and Ministry of John E. Geiger

Forrest L. Marion

With My Last Breath: The Life and Ministry of John E. Geiger

Author contact: forrest.l.marion@gmail.com

ISBN 979-8-56-582392-9

Cover design by Danellen DeHuff

Interior design and typeset by Katherine Lloyd at theDESKonline.com

"Finally, brethren, whatever is true, whatever is honorable, whatever is right, whatever is pure, whatever is lovely, whatever is of good repute, if there is any excellence and if anything worthy of praise, let your mind dwell on these things."

– PHILIPPIANS 4:8

"For the LORD takes pleasure in His people; He will beautify the afflicted ones with salvation."

– PSALM 149:4

"The memory of the righteous is blessed. . . ."

– PROVERBS 10:7

Contents

Acknowledgments

I have incurred numerous debts to individuals whose kindness and assistance have been instrumental in bringing this work to completion. In the late summer of 2018—before any thought was given to a biography—John Geiger sat with me for two interviews totaling about three hours. Later, when the idea of a biography was birthed, John provided me with his suggested names for interviews and contact information. All of John's recommendations plus several other interviews proved helpful.

Eastwood Presbyterian Church provided me with shared office space and a computer to work on the book—I thank our church administrator Jerry Knotts and deacon Bo Hodges. When, early in my work, the church's computers were hacked and the hackers demanded bitcoin to reestablish our files, Jerry—in fine Reaganesque fashion—told the hackers he did not negotiate with terrorists! (Thankfully, we had backup files.) Jerry also enabled me to sleep better at night knowing that he maintained multiple backups in the church office of all the interview audio files I gave him and the Word files of the slowly-evolving chapters.

In March 2019 I had the opportunity to spend a delightful Saturday evening and Lord's day at the home of John's oldest brother, Bruce, and his wife, Linda, in Visalia, California, just outside Sequoia National Park. We were joined by two other brothers: John's next-older-brother Steve; and younger brother Paul and his wife, Terrie. (The youngest Geiger brother, Greg, was in Hawaii with his family at the time.) Around the dining room table that Saturday evening, we called John and enjoyed a lively, lengthy conversation which was recorded as an interview. From then on, Bruce—the family historian—became my "go-to" Geiger brother for family background and information on John's early years as well as for his own remarkable story from Alaska. I am especially grateful for Bruce's numerous helpful responses and for his steady encouragement. Steve, who accompanied Bruce to Alaska in 1979, had kept a logbook of the trip, which proved quite useful. He also provided several beautiful photographs which John's family selected for use in the book. Greg and I talked on the phone and then met in person at John's memorial; he as well as Paul provided me with additional insights from their youth concerning John.

For those family members of John's, the Eastwood Christian School and Eastwood Presbyterian Church community, and friends of his from earlier years who sat for an interview, met or talked on the phone with me about John, or e-mailed or texted with remembrances, clarifying information, or answers to my questions, I thank you. Your inputs, even if brief or seemingly minor, were important to me. One friend in particular, Lawrence Kersten—a Fresno, California, native—whom John described as having walked with him in most of the seasons of his life, was especially helpful for filling in the knowledge gaps I had from John's years at Fresno State University.

In late 1991, John had spent several days at the cabin of his in-laws, Andrew and Syble Nolin, on Lake Jordan, Alabama, while praying through the decision of whether to go to Russia. In July 2020, I had the privilege to spend a full day at the same cabin while reading through the manuscript for John's book. I thank the Nolins for such a meaningful opportunity, as well as for allowing me to interview them about their son-in-law, whom they rightly considered *a son*.

For the considerable work involved in compiling the appendices—selecting several of John's songs, recipes, blog entries, and other family writings—I am grateful to Dawn, Soren and Virginia Geiger, Eric and Mary Agnes (Geiger) Walker, and Nolin Geiger; likewise, for their choosing the photos for the book. Although a teacher at heart, Dawn could easily find a career as an editor, and I am especially grateful for her superb editing—along with Soren—of the entire manuscript. Special thanks to Soren Geiger for selecting the typesetter (Katherine Lloyd) and printer and for coordinating the many details in the closing phase of the project; to Danellen DeHuff, an Eastwood teacher and church member, for her beautiful artwork on the front cover; and to Dr. Den Trumbull, for his encouragement and support, to include providing us with an unused ISBN number (an extra one from his own recent and valuable book on parenting).

I appreciate very much those who read and commented on the manuscript: Denise Brassell, Dawn Geiger, Soren Geiger, and Allen McDaniel. Many thanks also to Jeff Dunn for his feedback on a key section; Pastor David Lohnes for contributing the foreword; and Dr. Dominic Aquila for the back cover endorsement.

I'm grateful to my wife, April, for her gentle reminders that this book was to be more about John rather than about the school, although the two, of course, were tightly interwoven. To the extent the reader finds the focus to be where it ought—on John—you may thank April (as I do). I appreciate all those who provided encouragement along the way. Originally, I had hoped for a late 2021 completion, but in God's providence the Covid-19 shutdown of 2020 suddenly provided me with some three months to focus largely on this book. Most of all, throughout this process, I grew to love and appreciate my brother in Christ, John Geiger, more than I had before, and to be challenged by his example. John's words and example remain with me (including his final text to me on December 25, 2019); and I know I am not alone in such remembrances. As John put it, "Sin is a thief, faithfulness is a friend. Praise the Lord."

FOREWORD

Even though it meant a lot of organization, planning and logistics for us, I always looked forward, with anticipation, to the second week of March. We loved opening our home every year to the seniors from Eastwood Christian School. We were happy to meet new staff and renew old friendships, but truth be told, I was anxious to see John Geiger again. He was my friend, a longtime, intimate friend. Our friendship was mutual. My connection with John began long before our yearly encounters in France when we would travel together (with staff and students) to Normandy and visit the historic sites of the D-Day invasion. Never did we tire of returning to the same places, in particular the American cemetery, spread out on the bluff overlooking the sea and Omaha Beach where on June 6, 1944, two thousand U.S. soldiers were killed, wounded or went missing in action.

In late September 2018 one of John's longtime dreams came true. For what was to be their last time together, his four brothers joined him in France for a 3-day "tour" of Normandy. I, too, had the privilege of traveling with them to the coast; I was the chauffeur and the videographer, and so became a part of this final, memorable, Normandy-bound "Band of Geiger Brothers" adventure. I never had a brother, only two sisters. You'll understand my surprise when the evening before John's brothers returned to the States, they all five "officially," and unanimously, adopted me into the family as brother number six. So, I'm a Geiger now, and proud of it!

Before our visit to the American cemetery and the visitor information center, John gathered his brothers in close, around his wheelchair, and he spoke to us of the importance of virtue:

> This place is designed for the living as well . . . and that's you and me. You won't see it like you do here: examples of competence, courage, sacrifice . . . and there are more virtues that have been displayed on these beaches. Now these virtues are transferable for us in all our responsibilities, with your children, your wife, your home, your work and for the Kingdom of God. Every time I come here, I want to leave a more virtuous man—for the Kingdom of God.

I can't help but think of John as a kind of soldier, a warrior for sure! Like those brave men who stormed the beaches of Normandy in the face of what must have seemed insurmountable odds. He was always deeply moved by those noble virtues so evident in the stories of men and women who paid the ultimate price on foreign battlefields far away from home. I was deeply moved by those same virtues showcased in John's battle against the insurmountable odds of ALS during his last two years on earth.

John Geiger was a remarkable man, and he was as normal (human) as he was remarkable, but you had to spend time with him if you were to discover just how remarkable he was. I feel privileged to have done just that. He was a contagious *mélange* (mixture) of godliness and humanity. Although I already knew John for many years it was during his "dying years" that I learned so much from him about living.

My father was already in a coma when I finally reached home. He died shortly thereafter. My mother passed away 4 years later before we could even get back to Florida. John is the only person I have ever actually *journeyed* with, in an intimate, personal way, through "the valley of the shadow of death." His journey is over; no more valleys, no more shadows, no more death! The lessons I learned from him, however, left an indelible impression on me and will, I know, serve me well when my turn comes to walk through that final valley. Lessons about suffering, loss, disappointment, limitations, humility, faith, and hope. I had so many questions. He answered every one. "Thank you, John, for opening your heart to me, for *letting me in* and for displaying, in so many big and little ways, the non-negotiables of your faith in God and your unshakeable hope, so firmly anchored in the person and the promises of the resurrected Christ!

Did you know that 50 pairs of muscles and many nerves work to receive food into the mouth, prepare it, and move it from the mouth to the stomach? Did you know that there are 4 different stages of swallowing? Each time a different part of John's anatomy would succumb to the ravages of ALS he would do his research, proclaim his results and pronounce his conclusion, the same one every time: "David, our bodies truly are fearfully and wonderfully made!" Never once was I witness to him complaining that he could no longer walk, or talk, or swallow, or cook, play the guitar or piano, write songs, sing, or control his fluctuating emotions. Just . . . "Can you believe how fearfully and wonderfully we are made?"

On one occasion while he was staying with us in France, I asked John, "What is your biggest fear factor?" "No fear!" he replied without hesitation:

> Fear is the opposite of love. Love casts out all fear, fear has no place in a love relationship. They cannot coexist, one will always cancel out the other. On the other hand, what does make me sad is that I won't be around for my family, especially my grandchildren. They will only know me through stories and pictures. I'm being taken out of the dance, no longer an actor in the play. It's a small, temporary victory for "Death." I should have, long ago, recorded my songs and poetry for my family. I thought I would have my voice my whole life long. I thought I'd have use of my hands to play the guitar and the piano. But my voice is almost gone, and I can't play the piano or the guitar any longer. So, David, just do it! Now! Record that silly song and send it off to your grandkids. It doesn't have to be perfect or polished, they won't care, and it will be one more memory, one more *piece* of their *Papi*.

When my father found out from his doctor that he had 2 more years to live, the first words out of his mouth were, "Already? So soon?" He was 76 years old. Impending death redefines our purposes and our priorities. We would do well to listen carefully to what is said. John said some simple yet profound things to me that I will not soon forget:

> Enjoy people, stay put, build, grow. If you want to really be used, stay put. If you pull up a tree after a year and keep planting it elsewhere it will remain small. If you plant it in one place and leave it, it will grow tall and strong and bear much fruit.
>
> Take advantage of every breath, we all have limited breath, we just don't always know how long it will last. We assume it will last our whole life. I could be angry, bitter, upset, difficult to live with, prideful . . . or I can choose to rejoice in the Lord at all times, to be grateful and thankful. Ps. 118:24 says, "This is the day that the Lord has made, I will be glad and rejoice in it," and I will.
>
> Death is easy, life is hard! Lack of courage is nothing other than self-preservation and this is not attractive to Christ who said if you want to be my disciple you must die to self, take up your cross and follow me.
>
> When I was in Israel I drank freshly squeezed orange, pomegranate, and pink grapefruit juice. It was so delicious. I couldn't help but notice the pulp, and the way it had been literally crushed so that I could enjoy its delicious flavor. Our lives are like this. This is why Jesus is so sweet to those who "taste" Him . . . because He was crushed so completely . . . to a pulp. Out of His life comes the sweet taste of grace and forgiveness, eternal life and the Holy Spirit. When I got back from Israel, I told my family that the best thing I saw there was that juicer with the pulp, so they bought me one. Now every time I make juice, I think about the crushing that is necessary for me to enjoy that delicious fruit drink. Jesus was crushed on the cross and we need to be willing to be crushed, too, so that the sweet life of Jesus can be seen and tasted by the world around us. We need to be a peculiar people. Not angry, not bitter, not vengeful, not scared. Different! Jesus said that we need to take part in His suffering.

> The world needs to see us being crushed, broken and then they need to see and experience the sweet life of Jesus that is produced in us through our crushing.

One conversation in particular stands out to me as remarkable. He repeated to me on several occasions, "I will not disappear." I didn't understand what he meant, so I asked him to explain. Here was his reply:

> Inhibition is bondage! It makes one self-conscious, ashamed, embarrassed and unable to act in a relaxed and natural way. Freedom means no more hiding away hoping that no one will see me like this, hoping that no one will see my weakness, my handicap, my deteriorating body. The only other option is to become *invisible*, to *disappear*! To hide away! My role in God's vast plan is to still play my part in advancing His eternal cause; love the people He loves and share our hope in Christ. We have a choice to make as men when everything we depend on is stripped away. Men are proud, selfish, independent, and insecure. It's hard to be a man in our world today. We like to prove our worth, show off our strength, our talents, our capabilities. We want to be in control, and we want others to admire us; our skill, our beauty, our success! So, what happens when it's all stripped away and we need a walker or a wheelchair, we have to depend on others to clean up after us, we can't eat and talk at the same time because we'll choke. We spontaneously cry or laugh out loud over the silliest of things because we can no longer control our emotions. Our body is dying and it's ugly. Only two choices remain for a man; choose to remain engaged, to love others, to not be ashamed, to realize that at one point or another everyone is broken and ugly because of sin. This body isn't me, I'm a prisoner in this body, but until my last breath is gone, and even afterwards, I will bless others, listen to them, encourage them, love them, and tell of God's goodness and faithfulness. Or . . . I can "*disappear*." Out of shame I can lock myself away

behind nursing home doors and forbid that anyone come and see me in my condition. I can hide away, lonely and alone where nobody can see me anymore, and no longer be a man! To disappear is maybe the easier of the two decisions by far, but it's not the godly, courageous, admirable choice of a man. How sad to just disappear when God can use our brokenness and ugliness to showcase His goodness and grace. One of the positive byproducts of ALS is my total lack of inhibition. When I was younger, I evaluated everything through the lens of my own insecurities. I now have new freedom to love people outside of my own human insecurities because I don't have anything else to offer. I'm dying of ALS, I'm incapable of putting on a show or of "putting my best foot forward." What makes me valuable now? I can love, and smile and offer grace. I have no more insecurities. I am totally free to love and be present and actively participate in God's purposes for me, in me, and through me.

Although he talked about it a lot (to others, especially), John never seemed overly preoccupied with dying. He was, however, determined to use his impending death as an opportunity to publish and proclaim the glory of God! The group Urban Doxology sings a song entitled "Purge Me," which will always make me think of John:

I'm crying out, I'm desperate for you
I'm not afraid to open my heart and give you all
We'll declare your name, Jehovah reigns despite our problems
And through the pain we'll learn to trust in you.

John died from Lou Gehrig's disease on the 7th of January 2020. Soon after his diagnosis in the summer of 2017 churches began inviting him to tell his story. So, began "The Reflections of a Dying Christian." Invitations continued coming in. John's personal commitment to give testimony to God's glory sparked what became known as his "With My Last Breath Tour" which ultimately took him to Europe and Asia and beyond as he responded "yes" to every invitation. The song, "With My

Last Breath," composed and sung by John during the beginning stages of the disease became the theme song for his tour, as well as a moving memorial to his life.

Is it possible to make dying with ALS look "easy"? Of course not! Nonetheless, John helped me look past the ravages of his disease and see Christ. On occasion while talking with him, I literally felt like I was "sitting at the feet of Jesus." He would go take a nap, and I would run into my office and type out everything he said. I have five pages, single-spaced, of "Geiger Gleanings." He was an inspiration to me. Writing about him feels like an understatement. I'm grateful for the blessing of having known him beyond the limitations of descriptions, stories and words. I am a better man for it. His death was far from sudden but saying good-bye to John came far too soon!

In the following pages of this short biography, may you come to know John Geiger as a faithful warrior of Jesus Christ, and like me, may you be a better man (or woman) for it.

David V. Lohnes
Le Deluge, France
August 15, 2020

Preface

In August and September of 2018, I visited John and Dawn Geiger's home on two occasions for the purpose of interviewing John about his life. My friend and fellow elder in our church had been diagnosed with ALS (Lou Gehrig's disease) a year earlier. We had gone to lunch several times that year and enjoyed fellowship during this period in which John's symptoms were not severe enough to keep him from most of his regular activities. During the 2017-2018 academic year, John continued teaching and serving as the headmaster of Eastwood Christian School (ECS), where he had first begun teaching in the fall of 1997. As a military historian I had conducted hundreds of audio- or video-taped interviews with military members, later using some of them in publications. I knew that many of those who knew and loved John—myself included—would deeply regret the failure to record his unique story before it was too late. But I wasn't thinking of a biography at that point, I simply wanted to capture John's story for posterity. As I spent time with John and learned more of his life's story and ministry over the years, however, sometime during the fall of 2018 I suspect the Holy Spirit gave me a gentle nudge such that I began to reflect that to do a biography on John was not all that different from the three books I'd already done for the military—each of which depended heavily on oral history interviews. I shared the idea with a few others, all of whom encouraged me in it. By December I was ready to commit, and I asked John and Dawn if they would agree to allow me to take up the project, which required considerable commitment on their part as well. They said yes. This book is the result.

The work herein is by no means an in-depth biographical treatment. It is a somewhat brief and in many ways a superficial attempt to offer to its readers a glimpse of the life, character, ministry, and impact of a remarkable man whom I had the privilege to know, if not exceedingly well, yet well enough to offer the foregoing chapters in good faith. Having recently read highly-regarded biographies of Bernard Schriever, George S. Patton, Jr., and—dare I admit it—Maximilien Robespierre, I am aware of my own inexperience and limitations as a biographer. As a military historian I had not delved into this genre that calls for intense, focused attention and deep understanding of a single individual's makeup, career, relationships, and influence. Perhaps the present work may be of assistance to a later, more in-depth, treatment of John's life and ministry. Nonetheless, it is my prayer that even such a brief work as this, offered in a timely manner to the family, school, and church circles of John Edwin Geiger and to the broader communities of Montgomery, Alabama, Visalia, California, and places between and beyond—including many individuals overseas whose lives were touched by our brother—will be found to have value and to be of encouragement. If this little book serves to motivate one to seek the Lord Jesus Christ more closely as a result of reading of John's four-decade journey of walking with Christ by faith, it will have served its purpose more than I could have expected. And to God be the glory.

During one of the interviews for the book, a colleague of John's discussed with me his boss's unique communication skills, including John's willingness to be silly at times in order to gain the attention of his students. (This often meant assuming the persona of Quasimodo, Zeus, a medieval bard, or a rabbi.) Later, when I mentioned that discussion with John, he wrote the following to me:

> Ha. I have worn quite a few costumes over the years. I always tried to take the responsibility for communication. People come to classes . . . with so many dynamics holding them back from learning. They are weary and distracted. I think a speaker needs to make use of prosaic and oratorical techniques which reflect the image of man. Of course, Jesus really did model this. When using appropriate style, it is a way to say to the audience, "I love and respect you." Great writers *without oratory* should allow

> the audience the grace of letting them go home and read the message. Great oratory *without content* leads to manipulation and those speakers should be shunned. God's men and women should strive for both! For His glory and kingdom![1]

Even though his observations were thoughtful and refreshing, John followed up with, "Wow, I got on a bit of a soapbox. Sorry about that."

The heart of John's ministry was the twenty-one years he spent with Eastwood Christian School (1997-2018), the last sixteen and a half years as the headmaster. Some readers will note the omission of certain church matters during the middle years of John's tenure. Because those matters—unfortunate, but necessary to be dealt with by the church elders (the session, of which John was a member)—affected the school only indirectly, and as John was not as closely involved in them as were several other elders, those issues have been passed over in silence so as neither to detract from the book's main purpose nor rekindle controversies unlikely to be resolved at this point.

John's gifts were many and varied; readers will see numerous examples. But he had a few weaknesses, too. It was no secret to those in certain positions at ECS that John rarely got his grades in on time. One well-placed observer mentioned in passing that John "didn't know anything about grade books." Simply put, school administration—including financial matters—was not his gift or focus. His heart was elsewhere. To say that he could have, and should have, done better in those areas, generally, is a valid criticism. As has been rightly said, all men have feet of clay; and, from the inspired psalmist, "Do not trust in princes, In mortal man, in whom there is no salvation" (Psalm 146:3).

As the book neared completion, one incident that came to my attention illustrated a degree of administrative inattention on John's part. But, even more importantly, the incident highlighted John's consistent willingness to listen to a complaint and when convinced that it was valid, to act upon it. Around 2013-2014, the school's grass began to be cut by the son of an Eastwood church member. Often, the young man

1 E-mail, [subject unknown], John E. Geiger to author, Feb. 23, 2019.

found the grassy area around the ECS outdoor break area to have litter strewn about, hindering the grass-cutting because the trash first had to be picked up. The young man's father knew John well from church as well as ECS and spoke to him about the trash problem. John listened. Nothing seemed to improve. He brought it to John's attention again. The littering continued. This happened several times. Finally, in exasperation, the dad came to ECS one day, took a bag to the break area and filled it with the items he had picked up off the ground. He brought the bag into John's office—John was out at that moment—and deposited it on his desk. . . . From then on, the trash problem was no more. Later, John admitted to the dad his failure to resolve the problem in a timely manner. The two of them had butted heads over several things; the litter was only one of them. After its resolution, the two of them went on to a deeper friendship than they had enjoyed before, and in John's last year or two their fellowship gave much encouragement to both men.

Moreover, as the dad shared with me, John might easily have taken care of the difference of opinion by firing the young man—who no longer attended ECS—and hiring someone else to do the grass. To John's credit, he did not do that. Rather, John demonstrated the willingness, not only to listen to one who had been pounding him with a complaint, but, also, in the end to act with impartiality—a particularly difficult and often overlooked principle in Scripture.

During John's decade and a half as headmaster, he led a school based on the classical Christian model. An entry in the minutes of the Chowan Baptist Association (northeastern North Carolina) from the early nineteenth century, describing the qualifications for a pastor, offer insights for readers two centuries later who may be unfamiliar with the model:

> While we totally deny the necessity of a Classical Education as being essentially necessary to a Gospel Ministry, yet, under the teachings of the Holy Spirit, who will deny, that knowledge, almost of every kind, may be extensively useful to a Herald of Jesus. The increasing information among our brethren, the respectable talents of our adversaries, the veil that hangs over the best translation of Scripture, render such qualifications highly

> desirable. To be acquainted with Language and History, Natural and Moral Philosophy, the Mathematics and Rhetoric; and to be like Apollos, "*An eloquent man, and mighty in the Scriptures,*" is praise-worthy.[2]

Largely through self-study and practice, John Geiger became such a man. He consistently used opportunities in and out of the classroom—games, songs, and special events; senior speeches, devotional services, travel whether local or to Europe; and, perhaps most of all, day-to-day relationships, to promote the raising up of qualified heralds of Jesus among his students. But John was not a perfect man. He was a sinner redeemed by Jesus Christ, a man with a heart for people and the gospel of Christ. No one who knew him could honestly doubt that much.

In his last three years, John identified closely with a British Army brigadier from World War Two. Today, Brigadier Claude Nicholson of the British Expeditionary Force may be largely forgotten, but in May 1940 he and his men were directed by Churchill to "continue to fight" the Germans at Calais for as long as possible. Unlike other British forces, Nicholson's unit was not to be evacuated from the French coast even if it became feasible to do so. Every *hour* Nicholson and his men continued to exist, as the Prime Minister's wire stated, was of "the greatest help" to the Government. The brigadier was not privileged to know the reason for the order, but he wavered not and fought for a full 24 hours beyond the point at which resistance, militarily, had become useless. John drew great inspiration from Nicholson's story, and even in the midst of grievous afflictions in his last three years continued to fight as had the brigadier. Neither man had been given to know the full reason for his sufferings. In his ordeal of a different sort, John Geiger wavered not . . . even to his last breath.

Forrest L. Marion
Montgomery, Alabama
August 13, 2020

2 *Minutes of the North-Carolina Chowan Baptist Association . . . [May 22-24], 1819* (Norfolk, 1819), 14 [emphasis in original].

1

FAMILY

The Geiger and Pendola Ancestry

In the fall of 1948, Edwin Robert Geiger Jr. began classes at the College of the Sequoias, a two-year college in Visalia, California. He worked part-time at the Visalia Fox Theatre as an usher and assistant manager. The Fox had opened in 1930 and was described as "a smaller version of its more grandiose cousins in cities like Los Angeles."[1] Most likely, Robert—who went by his middle name—ushered more than a few patrons who came to see *Hamlet* (Laurence Olivier), *Red River* (John Wayne), or *The Treasure of the Sierra Madre* (Humphrey Bogart), three of Hollywood's biggest movies in 1948. Also that year, a high school senior named Dorothy Jean Pendola—a strawberry blonde and quiet by nature—worked evenings and Saturdays at the theater concessions booth. Their meeting at the Fox was the start of a relationship leading to 62 years of marriage, with an extended family of five sons and their wives, thirteen grandchildren, and more than seventeen great-grandchildren. In 1966, following Robert's Army service as a physician, Robert and Dorothy returned to Visalia and remained there for nearly fifty years. Ultimately, four of their five sons and their families spent many years in Visalia. Their middle son, John Edwin Geiger—the subject of this biography—was the lone exception.

1 "Visalia Fox Theatre," *www.cinematreasures.org*, accessed Aug. 2, 2019.

Both the Pendola and Geiger families had deep roots in Visalia, which in 1852 was said to contain between sixty and eighty inhabitants, as reported by surveyor Nathaniel Vise. Vise's ancestors hailed from Visalia, Kentucky, from which the new community—the oldest in the San Joaquin Valley between Los Angeles and French Camp (near Stockton)—took its name. Perhaps the next major event was the arrival of the telegraph in 1860.[2] The Pendolas, an Italian family originally from the Genoa area, had arrived in Visalia during the Gold Rush decade of the 1850s, traveling to California by wagon on the Oregon-California Trail network. Dorothy's grandfather—something of a roughneck according to family lore—was a merchant who ran a saloon and sold various goods to the miners in the area. When John recounted the family history, he noted that the Pendola side—in contrast to his father's straight-laced German ancestry—had "a lot of flair," including gunfights and stabbings in the store (or saloon). Dorothy's father worked as a truck driver, logger, and, in later years, as a bus driver. John's mother (Dorothy) was born in August 1931, the middle of three girls. The Pendolas also had one son.

The Geigers had emigrated to America from a fishing village on the Rhine River, in Bavaria (southern Germany). Arriving in the Chicago area in 1848, they joined the masses of newly-arrived Germans who flocked to the American Midwest to begin a new life free from the dangers of the revolutions and economic dislocations then threatening much of Europe. While the Geigers were farmers in the German community of Herscher/Reddick, Illinois, at least one Geiger son in a later generation tried something different. In early 1923, Edwin Robert Geiger Sr. partnered with a fellow German-American, Anthony Knittel, to secure a Ford garage in Herscher, but this enterprise lasted only six months. Looking for greater opportunities than farming in Illinois could offer them, Edwin and Marie Wilhelmina (Schlaich) Geiger packed up their two young children (Oren and LaRue) and moved to Visalia, where relatives of Marie's father had settled in the 1890s. Edwin and Marie had

2 "History of Visalia," Visalia, The Gateway to the Sequoias [website], www.visalia.city/about/history_of_visalia.asp, accessed Jun. 14, 2020.

visited the Schlaichs in Visalia only a year or two before, so the area was not a completely unknown undertaking for them.

When they arrived in Visalia, Edwin got a job washing cars at the Switzer Studebaker dealership, which was owned by a member of the German Lutheran Church in town. Edwin was good at repairing farm machinery and soon demonstrated his competence as an auto mechanic. Before long, his trustworthiness was such that he acquired the duty of traveling to San Francisco to secure new Studebakers and drive them back to Visalia. To pick up a new automobile, Edwin had to get to the Corcoran docks on Tulare Lake and take a flat-bottomed paddleboat north across the lake to the delta waters that led into San Francisco Bay. After picking up the Studebaker, on the drive back to Visalia—a trip of three days and two nights—he utilized the original U.S. Highway 99. (Interestingly, only a few years earlier during the U.S. Army's Punitive Expedition in Mexico chasing the outlaw Pancho Villa, Army elements including then-Lt. George S. Patton, Jr., a Californian, employed Studebaker automobiles. Family lore has it that John Geiger's great-uncle, Willie Schlaich, participated in that expedition, but supporting documentation has not been found.)[3] By the close of the 1920s, the couple added two more children to their family.

Of Ed and Marie's four children, three remained married for more than sixty years. All four children's marriages were parted only by death: Oren and Lucille had 65 years together; John and LaRue (Geiger) Hellenthal, 43 years until his death in 1989; Carl and Beverly (Geiger) Berg, 69 years; and Robert and Dorothy—John's parents—62 years. Especially in today's culture, four marriages—totaling 239 years—served as a remarkable reminder of the biblical intent for one man and one woman's marriage to not be torn asunder. The marriages pointed toward the considerable privilege, in today's parlance, of stable, intact households. Such long marriages also required God's blessing of longevity, reflected in the Ninetieth Psalm's "due to strength, eighty years."

Oren Geiger (1918-2013), the oldest of Edwin and Marie's four

3 Martin Blumenson, *The Patton Papers, 1885-1940, vol. I* (Houghton Mifflin Company: Boston, 1972), 378.

children, was ordained to the gospel ministry in 1945 as a Lutheran (Missouri Synod) pastor. Reverend Geiger served Grace Lutheran Church in Pittsburg, California, for nine years, and Good Shepherd Lutheran in Turlock, California, for thirty years. In addition to his pastoral labors, Oren served as local Rotary Club president and managed a championship Babe Ruth baseball team in the Northern California league. Oren and his wife, Lucille, had four children.

Ed and Marie's second child, LaRue (1920-2008), served in the Army Port and Service Command during World War Two, in Honolulu, where she met her future husband. In 1945, she married a second-generation Alaska resident and attorney, John S. Hellenthal. Her brother, recently-ordained Rev. Oren Geiger, officiated their wedding. (A half-century later, Oren's nephew, John Geiger, officiated several family weddings.) The couple settled in Alaska during an exciting time, which LaRue described: "That period, right after the war, was really a special time. Being an Alaskan meant that it didn't matter what your job was, what your religion was or what your political affiliation was; we all stuck together because we were Alaskans."[4] Alaska was still a territory, and in 1956 John Hellenthal was instrumental in drafting the constitution that led to Alaska's statehood three years later. John and LaRue had three children.[5]

The Geigers' younger daughter, and third child, was Beverly (1926-2018), who met her husband, Carl M. Berg, on a blind date while both were attending the University of California, Berkeley. They were married in 1948 and had three sons. For more than twenty years, Beverly taught at a Lutheran school in San Gabriel, California, where she and her husband lived for most of their married life.

Robert (1929-2015), the youngest, was born in Visalia as the Great Depression was beginning. Following pharmacy school and medical school, he served in the U.S. Army mainly as a surgeon before leaving the military in 1965 in order to pursue a civilian career as a general surgeon.

4 Biographical paper, LaRue Geiger Hellenthal, provided to the author by Bruce Geiger, Aug. 2019.

5 "Creating Alaska, John S. Hellenthal," University of Alaska, *www.alaska.edu*, accessed Aug. 3, 2019.

Following their courtship from about 1949, Robert and Dorothy (1931-2014) were married in February 1952, while he was in the middle of pharmacy school at the University of San Francisco. In 1953, Robert graduated and quickly joined the U.S. Army to take advantage of an opportunity to attend medical school at the University of California (San Francisco). While in medical school, Robert's family lived on the historic grounds of The Presidio, one of the most scenic spots in the Bay Area. During Robert's extended school years, John's two older brothers, Bruce and Steve, were added to the family. Bruce was born in November 1952, during Robert's pharmacy school studies; Steve, in 1955, when their father was midway through medical school. Many years later, Bruce could still remember hearing the fog horns of vessels in the bay especially during the summer months, reminiscent of Mark Twain's apocryphal quote that the coldest winter he ever spent was a summer in San Francisco.

John's Early Years

When John was born on November 13, 1958, the Geigers were on the cusp of several relocations in the next decade by virtue of Robert's Army career. Both John and his first younger brother, Paul (b. 1960), were born at Fort Lewis, Washington, the only two Geiger sons born in the same place. Bruce recalled the family lived on the Army post next to an infantry training area, which was almost their back yard. Bruce and Steve sometimes pulled John around in a little wagon, into which the older boys tossed expended ammunition cartridges they found on the ground. When the boys had gathered enough cartridges, they made belts out of the cartridges—just like the banditos they saw on television "Westerns" in that era.

Not long after Paul's arrival, in 1961 the family moved again, this time to Fort Campbell, Kentucky, where they lived for the next two years. Bruce, who turned ten while in Kentucky, recalled that during those years the brothers learned to rely on each other as their closest companions and did all sorts of things together. Because of moving so often, their friendships with other boys were always short-lived. Even as youngsters, they were becoming a "Band of Brothers." Bruce also remembered that as part of Fort Campbell's Armed Forces Day observance—the third Saturday in May—boys from as young as ten were allowed to fire several blanks from a .30-caliber machine gun. Pretty exciting for a young boy!

In a March 2019 gathering one delightful evening at the comfortable Visalia home of Bruce and his wife, Linda, three of the brothers concurred that their large family taught them to love one another even though "you may not like them" at times. For Bruce, one of those times might have been when he discovered that two of his younger brothers, John and Paul, had been pilfering his coin collection for their candy money. Bruce's clue to the fraternal criminal behavior was when he noticed pen marks on the inside of the cardboard coin folders next to the circular slots where his prized silver dimes and quarters had been inserted with care. John eventually broke down and confessed—Bruce didn't say what pressure had been applied. On another occasion—with John on the receiving end—youngest brother Greg put Tabasco sauce in the iced tea for John and several of his friends.

The fifth brother, Greg, was born early in 1964, the only one born in Visalia, where Robert and Dorothy settled the family before Robert's leaving home for a 12-month tour of duty in the Republic of Korea. Stationed in the city of Pusan, Dr. Geiger served as commanding officer of the Eighth U.S. Army's 11th Evacuation Hospital. During his time in Korea, he treated both U.S. military personnel and Korean civilians, including performing amputations on some of those badly injured by landmines left in the ground from the fighting between 1950 and 1953. In 1963, it was only a decade since the armistice that (mostly) ceased the hostilities between North and South Korea, and the South was only beginning to rise above the devastation left by decades of occupation and conflict.[6] In addition, there was the constant threat of a renewed attempt by the communist North to take over the fledgling republic in the South. For such reasons, very few U.S. military personnel were allowed to bring their families to Korea.

6 For one of several examples of North Korean acts of aggression some years after the armistice, see Forrest L. Marion, "A Hot Day in a Cold War: An RB-47 vs Mig-17s, April 28, 1965," *Air Power History*, vol. 53, no. 3 (Fall 2006), 26-33.

Visalia was to become the Geigers' long-term home, but not just yet. One clear remembrance of Bruce—who turned eleven in November 1963—was the assassination of President John F. Kennedy that month. When Robert returned stateside from Korea, the family moved all the way across the country, to Fort Devens, Massachusetts. Second-oldest brother Steve recalled being exasperated at John when, during the commercial flight east, John *slept* instead of enjoying the fantastic view from the air. The Geigers' time in New England was very short, however, as Robert decided to leave the Army and enter private practice.

In June of 1965, the Geigers moved to the small town of Whitefish, Montana (not yet a tourist attraction). There, Robert served largely as an old-fashioned country doctor, delivering babies and caring for those with mostly common ailments. As in olden days, it was not uncommon for Dr. Geiger to be paid for his medical services not in cash but with firewood, chickens, or potatoes picked from a family's field. John remembered that during this time he saw his father serving others with a gracious spirit, which no doubt influenced his sons as well. Even so, the life of a country doctor was not what Robert wanted for a career. He was trained as a surgeon and wanted to find a place to put those skills to use. The Geigers lived in Montana for only five months before moving on to Reno, Nevada.

In later years, the five brothers agreed that John, as the middle son, generally "blended in" and passively acquiesced to what others wanted to do. In 2018, John recalled that in his youth he was not a "strong personality," and he sought to avoid conflict. He wanted to be liked. He would "put up with whatever" and would choose his fights sparingly. His passive nature was something he was to work on in later years, assisted by his wife, Dawn. John's older brothers, Bruce and Steve, also remembered John's childhood nickname of "Bombalini" (also "Bombus"). If a glass had been broken in the Geiger home, it was usually John's doing.

The year of 1965-1966 was perhaps the most difficult for the Geigers, at least in one way: they moved three times in ten months—from Massachusetts to Montana, from there to Nevada, and, finally, back to Visalia where they were to settle for good. John's nearest-in-age younger brother, Paul, was in three different kindergartens during the school year.

The move produced some unique pressures and circumstances as well. John recalled that after being in Reno at Christmastime, 1965, the family arrived back in Visalia by the spring. School was still in session, and John was a second grader. November was John's birth month, so he had missed celebrating his birthday at the Visalia school where each student enjoyed a class party for his or her birthday. In the spring of 2019, John shared a confession:

> I was not going to be able to have a class party, so I lied to the teacher and told her my birthday was in the summer, July 3. I had the party and right before they sang the teacher asked me to give my birthdate to the class. I said July 4th. Darwin Dixon stood up and called me out as a liar. All hell broke loose and I was melting up front, caught in a second grade lie. Years later Darwin was driving by the Laurel house [the Geiger family home] and stopped to say hi. I retold the story and told him that guilt [had helped] point me to Christ.[7]

John added that it was a "great way to finish a traumatic event from childhood."

7 E-mail, John E. Geiger to author, "Re: Family timeline," ca. Mar. 6, 2019.

2

High School Years

In later years, John referred to himself as having been "a happy little kid," very inquisitive, generally acquiescing to the desires of others and avoiding conflict. He moved easily with the current of people around him, but there's a weakness in that, John reflected. In 2018-2019, his self-assessment was, "I was not and still am not a strong personality." In around the 6th grade, "I was introduced to the world of sin, deep sin," he recalled, including "boy-girl stuff" and profanity. From that time and through high school, John began squandering his life, he said, and all of it was outside the family circle; "my parents didn't really know."

John's years at Mount Whitney High School in Visalia were confusing for him. Looking back, John considered he had really wasted those years: "I was fairly intelligent, but I didn't apply myself." His friends must have thought John fairly intelligent, too, as they'd "cheat off of me." So he knew he was smarter than they were, but he was squandering his education. John's high school had more than a thousand students. Like many other teenagers, he joined with his school friends in carousing, especially on the weekends, including a lot of drunkenness, profanity, wasting time, and "just looking for excitement."

John participated in high school sports, although as he wrote many years later, "With the physical activity associated with a family of five boys, who needed school sports?" During his ninth grade football season, John recalled, with truthful humor, "I *practiced* football and watched the games; I had a great seat on the sideline." He was "fierce enough for the sport," but his miniscule size in those days made him most useful to his team "when the coach wanted to demonstrate a tackle."

Wrestling Years

With football a disappointment, John began wrestling that winter, where "I would compete against boys my own size, sort of." Moreover, the contest was one-on-one, with nobody else to blame. His oldest brother, Bruce, had wrestled four years at Mount Whitney and a year at the College of the Sequoias, so that sport was already familiar to John. Considerably huskier than his younger brothers, Bruce was known to wrestle all four of them at home, basically piling them into a big ball on the floor—and then sitting on them—to their parents' eye-rolls at the sight and sound of their younger sons' yells for Bruce to let them go. John grew in stature later than most of his peers. He was four feet, eleven inches going into 9th grade, "a tiny little guy," as he said. The lightest weight class was 95 pounds, but when he started high school he weighed only 87. So, for his first year, John wrestled *under* weight, a distinct disadvantage for a wrestler.

Decades later, as the Eastwood Christian School (ECS) headmaster, John shared a story from his 9th grade wrestling experience on the junior varsity. It went like this:

> One morning at school, halfway through the season, the varsity coach saw me in the hall and said, "Geiger, my man is sick, so you are wrestling varsity tonight." He didn't seem all that thrilled to have an inexperienced rookie filling in for his seasoned veteran. Gulp. I suddenly felt sick as well. Wrestle varsity? Not on the night when our opponents were the notorious Hanford Falcons! Fear gripped me in its talons. Then, the teasing began by my buddies. "Gonna be a tough night." "Heard the guy you're up against is a beast." "Did you know the Hanford guy [a senior] is

undefeated?" . . . I took all this with a laugh and didn't believe a word of it. Nobody is that good and I was scared enough just having to wrestle with all those upperclassmen.[1]

John recalled shaking hands with his opponent and thinking, just before the referee's whistle which was to begin the match, that he "looked taller and stronger than 97 lbs. should be." John's vivid remembrance continued:

> I was swooped up and thrown to the mat before I knew that the whistle had blown. A player receives 1 point for gaining control of his opponent, 2 points for reversing the control, and 2-3 points for almost pinning the opponent. A pin is when a wrestler's shoulders both touch the mat for two seconds. If you're pinned, the match is over. To prevent being pinned, a player usually bridges (arching the back and supporting oneself with the head, neck muscles, and possibly the elbows). In a matter of 6 seconds I was already down 4-0. I lay bridging for the entire first round . . . and the second . . . and the third. My memories . . . are hearing the fans yell, "Get up, John!" and the Hanford Falcon [coach] saying to the referee, "He has to be pinned by now!" and the ref saying, "No, not yet."[2]

The match ended in a humiliating 14-1 defeat, John gaining a point when the Falcon senior committed an illegal move (perhaps jumping on John's chest, as John recalled). The story concluded with:

> The referee pulled up the hand of the winner and kindly adjusted my dazed body so I would walk back to my bench. As I approached, my teammates were cheering and clapping. (*Teens can be cruel*, I thought.) The coach seated me beside him and the next match began. I couldn't bear to lift my head and watch.

---

1 John Geiger, "Last Breath Blog, Grappling with ALS," Feb. 17, 2019.

2 Geiger, "Grappling with ALS."

> At some point Coach Lloyd leaned over to me and said, "I am proud of you." . . . "That boy you wrestled has pinned everyone this season. You spoiled his record." I looked across the mat and saw the tall, muscular boy sitting with slumped shoulders and head down, disappointed. It is amazing how quickly one can go from shame to a sense of pride. I sat up and watched the rest of my teammates wrestle, enjoying my first experience as a varsity wrestler. Sometimes you win even though you lose.[3]

In 2019, an ECS 10th grader, Trey Hawkins, remembered that story and applied it to John's life in a conversation with him. Later, John wrote in his blog, "My body is losing its fight against ALS. Some days I feel like my only option is to sustain a bridge move as long as possible." He continued, ". . . though I lose in the body now, Jesus Christ's death and resurrection offers victory for my spirit and hope for a renewed body: '*We are more than conquerors through Him [Christ] who loves us.*' "

Such was one of the lessons God had for John as a high schooler that he was to appreciate as a grown man and a follower of Christ. In his second year of wrestling, as a 10th grader, he got up to 95 pounds and wrestled at that weight. As a junior, he wrestled at 103, and senior year, John had "fattened up to 133 [pounds]." John became competent as a wrestler but had a rebellious heart, he confessed.

Other Highs and Lows

Aside from school and sports, John was involved in other extracurricular activities. During their high school years, he and his brother, Paul, participated in the Future Farmers of America. In those years, Paul was the life of the party with his friends, which probably contributed to his graduating 364th in his class of 365. Although he struggled for several years, including an initial unsuccessful stint at the College of the Sequoias, in 1981 Paul returned to college, having learned to read much better than before, and made the President's List. Later, he earned

3 Geiger, "Grappling with ALS."

a master's degree from Northwestern University and went on to own a prosthetics company—a prime example of a late-bloomer.

John also was drawn toward other outdoor activities and adventures. He and Bruce frequented an area east of town called Lemon Cove where they hiked, camped, and shot rabbits and quail. The Geigers even reloaded their own ammunition at home. Bruce recalled that John became pretty good at the "trickspin" technique with a .41-caliber Ruger six-shooter. As a surgeon, their father was often busy with his patients, so there were times when, on her own, Mrs. Geiger took the boys on the short drive from their home to a scenic spot in the mountains for a big campfire breakfast.

By John's senior year, 1975-1976, things started catching up with him. That fall, he quit the football team because the coach wouldn't play him, and he managed to get himself kicked off the wrestling team that winter. From John's perspective, he was tired of wasting his time. That year, John also had a car accident, his girlfriend dumped him, and school got harder:

> I was ditching school and my grades. On all fronts I was coming to grips with my brokenness and self-destructiveness . . . the lack of joy, the lack of meaning, purpose, *I really hated life.* I spent a night in jail, being mischievous, just messing around with fire hydrants. The cops knew a good night in jail will wake a kid up. . . . [I had] a lot of self-destructive behavior.[4]

John might not have known it at the time, but it was Bruce's idea to give John the night in jail. Their parents were out of town when the incident occurred, so after Dr. Geiger took the phone call from the police station, he called Bruce at home. Bruce—whether by wisdom beyond his years, or perhaps not wanting to be bothered with his younger brother—recommended that instead of bailing John out, they let him spend the night in jail. And that's what happened.

John planned to attend the College of the Sequoias after high school.

4 Interview, John E. Geiger with author, Montgomery, Ala., Aug. 10, 2018.

He ended up taking the ACT exam the day after being slightly injured in a car wreck. Bruce remembered that shortly after the accident he saw John with a fat lip—which was not uncommon for the brothers. John recalled taking that test: "I remember shading [filling] in bubbles, making patterns" with the answers. When the scores came in, a school official sat him down and asked, apparently in all seriousness, "With this ACT score, how did you graduate from high school?" John told him, "'I basically guessed.' . . . I had a fat lip . . . I didn't care . . . it was my prideful independence." Soon, John was to begin taking life more seriously.

3

A New Creation

[Note: The first two paragraphs below are John Geiger's own words as recorded on Aug. 10, 2018, at the Geiger home in Montgomery, Alabama. With permission of Dawn Geiger, minor edits to the actual words spoken have been made for ease of reading.]

> "During the first year of college, that's when God really moved in on my life. I was in church, I was raised a Lutheran, and it was fairly boring from my perspective. I used to sleep a lot in church, and one day, when I was maybe a senior, I was a little embarrassed to go to sleep. So I grabbed a book to try to wake up; I grabbed the pew Bible. I figured I'll look at the maps. . . . *No maps!* So, I randomly flipped through and my eyes fell on—I didn't really know the name of the book—but it was Galatians 5, verse 19, which talks about the deeds of the *flesh*. And there was a list of actions. Some of the words I didn't know what they meant . . . but the ones I did know, drunkenness, immorality, outbursts of anger, carousing, I realized, huh, that's me, that's my life, it's what I do in my free time. And then the writer said, '*Those who practice such things, like I said before, will not inherit the kingdom of God.*' That woke me up. I was a church-goer, I figured I was going to heaven. The Holy Spirit made me honest that

day. And I had the fear and the knowledge that I was going to hell. I probably escaped death two or three times that year and I realized that hell—I had a vivid enough imagination and enough biblical instruction to know—hell was *forever*. And I was scared. For a year and a half, two years, I checked *every* Bible I had time to look at, making sure that verse was still there."

"I was with my classmates on a field trip, in San Luis Obispo, and I pull out the Gideon Bible, *there it is* [the verse], and I remember reading it to my buddies in the room, and saying, 'Guys, what do you think? This is what we do.' I remember one of them said, 'John, ask for forgiveness, you're all right. God understands, as long as you say you're sorry, you can live that way.' Something inside of me didn't buy that, but I was definitely under conviction of the Holy Spirit, and I was ready when our associate pastor [Gene Antonio] showed up, talking about the *blood of Christ* that washes our sin away. I listened to those sermons, and I was born again then. . . . I really went through, scripturally, what they call becoming a new creation. God started purging and cleaning my lifestyle, my habits, my mind, my language. I was born again. I had a lot of residuals, still do, junk, but I was undoubtedly a new creature. My friends rejected me for the most part. I was not obnoxiously evangelistic, I just wasn't one of them anymore. . . . [John was at the College of the Sequoias by this time, where he attended from 1976-1978; most likely, these developments fell between late 1977 and early 1978]. I was a pre-med, doing very well in the science world. I was considering a third year because a professor wanted me to be a TA [teaching assistant]. I wasn't in a hurry, I was young . . . I wanted to help people."

Looking back on those years at the age of fifty-nine, John realized he had been learning to obey his conscience, increasingly informed as it was by the Bible. Late one night, he walked into his younger brother Paul's room—after sliding the door open as loudly as he could, as older brothers are wont to do—arousing him from an alcohol-induced slumber. In very basic terms, John told Paul he was going to hell, that he needed Christ, and to repent. Probably still fuzzy-headed, Paul acknowledged his brother's counsel and then asked if he could go back to sleep. John returned to his room and did the same. Many months later, while listening to Paul's testimony during a Bible study and fellowship at the Geiger home, John learned that the Holy Spirit had used their late-night encounter to begin a gracious work in Paul's heart.

In addition to Gene Antonio's ministry that focused on Christ's gracious giving of Himself for sinners, Grace Lutheran's associate pastor was instrumental in John's life. Known affectionately as "the Italian Stallion" and "Gene, Gene, the Christian Machine," he got John and others into studying the Bible, prison ministry, and handing out evangelistic tracts. With Gene's encouragement, for a time John hosted a local radio program in Visalia—fifteen minutes a week—called the "Quarter Hour of Power." Gene taught young believers in Christ, like John, that being radical isn't always a bad thing. But he also gave a book to John. It was a collection of sermons by the nineteenth century Baptist pastor, Charles H. Spurgeon. Soon, John was devouring Spurgeon's sermons at the rate of one every few days. His love of Spurgeon, and later, of other like-minded theologians, was to become the catalyst for a deep, lifelong friendship with a brother-in-Christ named Lawrence Kersten.

4

Alaska John

As John grew into young manhood, his love of the outdoors grew as well. Living in Visalia, known as the Gateway to the Sequoias, he had plenty of opportunities to pursue hunting, fishing, and archery. Years later, John shared that one of his fears about Christianity during his high school years was that he'd have to give up such adventures in order to follow Christ. In 2019, John recalled that following his conversion, the first section of the Bible he read was the Book of Acts—the adventure-filled narrative account of the spread of the gospel in the period following Christ's death, resurrection, and ascension. From his reading of Acts, John said he quickly began learning that "Christians can really live on the edge." John reflected that he had been privileged to have some forty years of walking with Christ, observing, "Faithfulness to Christ is worth it. . . . Sin is a thief, faithfulness is a friend. Praise the Lord."

Bruce and Steve's Adventure

But John was not the only Geiger brother to experience the rigors of outdoor adventure as a young man. Bruce experienced one of the family's most dangerous incidents, if not the one closest to a fatal outcome. In 1978, John's 25-year-old brother picked up and moved from Tulare, California, to Alaska, influenced in part by the quasi-frontier experience of his Uncle John and Aunt LaRue Hellenthal's long-term residence there. If he was looking for a little excitement, he was to get it! Bruce and Steve—who had just quit his quality control job at the Foremost Foods' ice cream plant in San Francisco and was readily available—took a more remote highway than most who drove from the U.S. Pacific Northwest to Alaska. Instead of using the popular Alaska-Canadian (Al-Can) highway, for a good portion of the trip they took the Cassiar Highway (British Columbia Highway 37), the farthest northwestern highway in the Canadian province of British Columbia (B.C.). The Cassiar promised a more adventuresome experience, one worthy of Bruce's brand-new 440 Dodge 4x4 Ram Charger. On September 11th, Bruce drove from his home to Steve's apartment in San Francisco; his brother piled in, and they headed north.

The trip was an unforgettable eleven days, filled with beautiful scenery—it was *a hoot*, Bruce recalled. They camped out at night along the way. After crossing into Canada, they spent one night at Lytton, B.C., and from there they continued north to Prince George. On their sixth night out, at Kitwanga Lake, a friendly outdoorsman warned them not to set up their tent in a low-lying area. They ended up going fishing with him and caught eight "cut-throat trout," Steve recalled. They enjoyed trout for dinner for the next several nights. From Kitwanga—roughly halfway through British Columbia from south to north—they hopped onto the Cassiar (Highway 37) and remained on it all the way to Watson Lake, Yukon Territory. At one point a bush pilot flying a small, high-wing aircraft circled overhead and then landed behind them on the gravel-packed road. The pilot soon taxied up and joined them at the gas station on the side of the road to refuel. It was the lone station for many miles.

At Watson Lake, they rejoined the Alaska Highway (Highway 1) and continued westward through Whitehorse and on to the Canadian-U.S. border. On the eighth day they entered Alaska, but it was still three more days to Anchorage, where the Hellenthals lived. Their uncle and aunt kindly had them stay with them for a month or so while their nephews began looking for work. Bruce had expected to make contact with a friend in the crabbing business, but—in the days before cell phones and the internet—his buddy, Jack Prince (his real name), was not so easy to track down. The brothers even took a commercial flight to Kodiak to look for Jack but failed to find him. When they returned, Bruce started a job at a creamery in Anchorage—the same type of work he had done in California. Steve began a job at a convenience store in town.

Sirius Saga and Survival

The brothers spent Christmas 1978 with the Hellenthals. After finally locating the elusive Jack, Bruce landed a job on a crabbing boat owned by Seward Fisheries, the 83-foot *Sirius*. Little did he know that January was a time of year when the local waters were among the roughest, including high swells, high winds, snow, and ice. Typically, *Sirius*, manned by a crew of six, conducted a triangular crabbing route, leaving port at Homer and working her way toward Seward, then on to Kodiak and back to Homer. On the last day of February, *Sirius* had just off-loaded a catch at Seward and was proceeding toward Kodiak through the Shelikof Strait.

On the evening of February 28th, winter storm conditions threatened those vessels near Cape Douglas at the north end of the Strait. At about eight o'clock, Bruce was at the wheel directing *Sirius* on a southwesterly course toward its submerged crab pots when suddenly the boat struck a portion of Douglas Reef. He recalled, "All of a sudden we hit the reef and everybody was out of their bunks." *Sirius* had run aground an hour before low tide. Initially, the crew hoped that the imminent rising tide would lift her from the reef. But the high winds and waves "slammed the grounded boat into the rocks," as the *Times-Delta* reported.[1]

Although *Sirius* reported she had run aground, at first the captain did not think he required U.S. Coast Guard assistance due to the tide. In any case, another vessel, the 90-foot *Sea Wife*, was in the vicinity attempting to help *Sirius*. But even after several passes, *Sea Wife* was unable to get a line on the distressed vessel, whose bow was under the water by that time. By then, *Sirius* had requested assistance from the Coast Guard, which launched a Sikorsky H-52 rescue helicopter and a four-engine C-130 Hercules transport. The Air Force's rescue service followed suit, launching a larger, twin-engine Sikorsky H-3 helicopter and

1 Tom Ruppel, "Visalian Tells Chilling Tale," *Visalia Times-Delta*, Mar. 1, 1979.

a rescue-modified C-130 twenty minutes later. But the slow-flying helicopters were more than two hours away. Meanwhile, a larger vessel, the 179-foot *Polar Shell*, arrived on scene and sent its diver into the freezing water to try to attach a line to *Sirius*. Around midnight the engine room began taking on water, yet another turn for the worse. Bruce, who had borrowed his father's prized Kelty (down-filled) sleeping bag, went back into the berthing area to try and retrieve it. Forty years later, Bruce also remembered that as *Sirius*'s plight worsened he thought of some of the World War Two movies he had watched as a boy in which a ship was torpedoed and goes down as a result. . . . Now it was happening to him, or so it seemed. And if the situation was not grim enough, Bruce had decided *not* to spend the hefty sum of three hundred dollars for a waterproof survival suit. Without it, his time of useful consciousness in the freezing water would be very short, indeed, no more than a couple of minutes. He put on as many layers of clothing as he could, but had he ended up in the water, they would only have weighted him down.

At 1:25 am, the plucky, single-engine H-52 helicopter arrived overhead and went into a demanding nighttime over-water hover above the sinking *Sirius*, lowering a rescue basket to the now mostly submerged deck. (A nighttime, overwater hover—without visual references—is one of the most demanding maneuvers for a helicopter pilot and crew.) Somehow, the small helicopter picked up not only all six crew members of *Sirius*, including Bruce Geiger, but also the *Polar Shell*'s diver. Based on the Coast Guard's official public information release, the *Kodiak Daily Mirror* observed that "it was something of a feat for the small H-52 helicopter to pick up seven people." Perhaps just as impressive, there were none injured among the rescuees. But others were not so fortunate that night. Bruce recalled having heard a "Mayday" radio call from two other vessels, and the talk the next day was that at least two boats had gone down in addition to *Sirius*. One of the other vessels probably was the 139-foot *Alaska Roughneck* which ran aground and rolled over in Cold Bay near King Cove. Two of its crew of four perished.[2]

2 [article title unknown, excerpt provided to author by Bruce Geiger], *Kodiak Daily Mirror*, Mar. 1, 1979; Ruppel, "Visalian Tells Chilling Tale," *Visalia-Times Delta*, Mar. 1, 1979;

Following the loss of their crabbing vessel, Bruce and Jack showed up at Steve's apartment. Steve, who knew nothing of the wreck or the rescue at sea, was shocked not only by their harrowing account but also by Bruce's loss of weight. Years later, Steve remembered that when he first saw Bruce he thought he resembled their younger and smaller-framed brother, Paul. To celebrate their survival, if not also for Bruce to put back on a few of the pounds he had lost, he and Jack flew to the Hawaiian island of Maui for a much-needed recuperation. Bruce lost his wallet and savings when the *Sirius* sank, but the captain kindly gave him a couple hundred dollars to help him out. Bruce stayed two weeks, then flew home to California. For a time, he thought of returning to Alaska, because as he said forty years later, you could "make Big Bucks up there *if you live*." Instead, he opted to stay in Visalia, influenced by a growing romantic relationship with a young woman he had been writing (people wrote *letters* in those days). Bruce and Linda were married on March 1, 1980. While the wedding date was not planned with the anniversary in mind, it was one year to the day after Bruce's life-saving rescue.

Resettling in Visalia in 1979, initially Bruce tried his hand as a California real estate agent. Realizing that was not for him, he transitioned into insurance, becoming an agent with an insurance company for Lutherans, which he found to be a much better fit.

Steve and John's Trip Home

Meanwhile, after Bruce's decision to fly home from Maui, Steve was given the responsibility of getting his brother's Dodge Ram Charger back to Visalia. To help Steve with the long and potentially hazardous trip, John received a directive from his parents to fly up to Anchorage and join him for the journey home. John was in his first year at Fresno State University. He would have to miss a week of school and spend his Spring Break on the excursion. John recalled that one of his professors, George Diestel, was upset that John was to miss a week of class. John told him, "Sorry, family trumps schooling." What he failed to confess was that "*a whole lot*

Alaska Shipwrecks website, "Alaska Commercial Fishing and Other Maritime Losses of 1979," February 28, 1979, at *alaskashipwreck.com* (accessed Oct. 5, 2019).

of things trumped schooling" for John in those days. Upon John's return, his professor dubbed him, "Alaska John." John liked the nickname.

During his short time in Alaska, John stayed with the Hellenthals. His Uncle John showed him part of downtown Anchorage where the road had dropped about six feet as a result of the earthquake of March 27, 1964; the epicenter had been eighty miles from Anchorage. At least one hundred thirty persons died and property damages tallied more than 300 million dollars (1964 USD). The city had determined the repairs at that particular spot in Anchorage were too expensive to make, and they left the site as a reminder of the great earthquake.

Steve's logbook entry showed it was the last day of March when he and John set out for Visalia. From Anchorage, they drove on a snow-packed road for two-and-a-half days to get to a ferry at Haines, Alaska, which was to carry them to Seattle. Once while John was driving, they lost traction and slid into a snow bank, but emerged unscathed. Of the drive to Haines, John remembered there were no telephone poles along the road and there were bald eagles "by the dozens." Steve remembered seeing moose as well. The accommodations on the ferry were spartan—it was more a cargo than a passenger vessel—which, according to John, "made the adventure more adventurous." There was a lot of fog and mist while traveling through the inland passage, and the scenery "was wild, rugged, and breathtaking." Steve had bought a couple of down-filled vests to keep warm on the trip, a green one for John, a blue one for himself. In late 2019—by which time it was exceedingly difficult for John to type out any e-mail or message—he wrote to the author a lengthy reply, including: "I still have the vest. I gave it to Soren last year and he uses it to this day. We disembarked in Seattle and drove nonstop to Visalia."

On a Lord's day afternoon in the fall of 2019, members of the Eastwood church choir sang at the Geiger home, and the author, standing next to John, was privileged to read the draft of one of the book's early chapters to the gathering. Reminiscent of John's Alaska days, Soren wore the vest. Although by 2019 John's days of outdoor adventure had passed, he was still living for Christ "on the edge."

5

Bonding Over Spurgeon

In the fall of 1978, nineteen-year-old John Geiger began classes at California State University, Fresno, often referred to as Fresno State. As Fresno was only about an hour's drive from his home in Visalia, he commuted. Although he was young in the Christian faith, already John was more inclined toward ministering to the needs of soul rather than body. By this time, he was leading a weekly Bible study in the Geiger home with up to fifty or sixty young people packed into the living room area. Prior to that year, John had considered following in his father's career path as a physician. In order to help prepare for the ministry, which involved the presentation of biblical truth in various settings, John decided to major in Communication.

In the late spring of 1979, a Communication major and Fresno native, Lawrence Kersten, heard about a student called "Alaska John." In time, Lawrence found himself at the university library facing an assignment that required him to do research on someone. He made a passing remark to several other students standing nearby, "I wish I could do some research on someone interesting . . . like Charles Spurgeon." John was among the students within earshot and immediately perked up at the mention of Spurgeon. "Oh, you read Spurgeon?" John queried. Indeed, Lawrence had begun reading of the life and ministry, as well as the sermons, of the nineteenth century English Baptist preacher, Charles Haddon Spurgeon.

Beginning a Lifelong Friendship

From that moment, John and Lawrence became close friends. Forty years later, John wrote in an e-mail that "friendships are formed when passions are shared." He also quipped that there were "not a lot of twenty-year-old Spurgeon Groupies out there" at Fresno State. Lawrence had grown up mostly unengaged in matters of faith, but a Baptist friend had invited him to some evangelistic meetings, which he attended. There, the thing that impressed Lawrence most of all was the seriousness his peers seemed to have toward the subject. In 2019 he recalled his attitude at the time had been, "You mean this stuff is true and you're supposed to pay attention?" And from that point, the Lord began a gracious work in Lawrence's heart, on the one hand revealing his sin and, on the other, convincing him from the Bible that by trusting in Jesus alone for pardon, he was thereby credited with Christ's perfect record (called justification). In the other half of the great transaction known as the gospel, Lawrence's own record of sin was credited to Christ. The apostle Paul described it in 2 Corinthians 5:21: *"He made Him who knew no sin to be sin on our behalf, that we might become the righteousness of God in Him."*

By the time Lawrence met the Alaska John he had heard about, he was already wrestling on his own with the practical working out of his faith in Jesus Christ. John was doing something similar as well. Lawrence described the basis of their long friendship:

> We bonded as young males becoming men, wanting to be genuine, authentic, Christian men who are not heretics, not ashamed of our lives. . . . We bonded over ideas . . . and we spent a lot of time talking about themes like justification, and sanctification . . . each of us would be reading something and we'd share it with the other. . . . We just took it seriously. . . . Each of us was a voracious enough reader that we were really

> wrestling with trying to do the right thing . . . [and with] who we were, and what the faith meant, how it all worked.[1]

Both of them were reading various thinkers and theologians in addition to Spurgeon, including A. W. Tozer and J. C. Ryle. John and Lawrence were building what they called "our great dead men's shelf," which consisted of the works of Christian writers, especially from nineteenth century Great Britain that had stood the test of time. In many of those books, they discovered *another world* in terms of "what was expected of the normal Christian life" in the previous century. A typical example was found in an 1820s' manual for Briery Presbyterian Church members, in rural Virginia, in which a question for self-examination asked, "Do you regularly and seasonably attend on the public worship of the congregation? Do you endeavor to *BE STILL*; to be attentive; frequently to lift up your heart to God during the service; to sing with the spirit, and the understanding, making melody in your heart?[2]

Lawrence added, "The great thing is . . . for both of us, we were bonding over really the most important thing in our life. . . . We weren't bonding over football or certain hobbies, we were really bonding over the thing about which we were the most passionate, [and] that was our faith." For those important discussions, the two often went to a favorite burger joint in Fresno called Spanky's, where they might spend two or three hours together. Going for a "Spanky burger" became a regular, much-anticipated, and fruitful time as John and Lawrence talked about life and how their faith impacted it. Sadly, in June 1982 Spanky's was robbed, and the proprietor was shot and killed during the robbery. John had just graduated from Fresno State, while Lawrence had one more year to finish his bachelor's degree. While their friendship continued, Spanky's had closed and so had the first and perhaps the most consequential chapter in John and Lawrence's relationship.

In later years, John settled in Alabama and Lawrence in Texas. Both

---

1 Interview, E. Lawrence Kersten with author, Dallas, Tex., Sept. 26, 2019.

2 *A Manual for the Members of the Briery Presbyterian Church, Virginia* (Richmond, Dec. 1828), 55.

found their spiritual home in the Presbyterian Church in America. John became the headmaster of a classical Christian school in Montgomery; Lawrence earned a doctorate in Communication and taught for a time before moving to Dallas. They sometimes coordinated their trips home to see their families in California so they also could see one another. In 2000, Lawrence got married. John, who had graduated from seminary and been ordained to the ministry, officiated his friend's wedding. Unknown to John at the time—and perhaps even at their last meeting in 2019 at the Geiger home in Montgomery—John had skipped a part of the ceremony. Lawrence and his bride had hired three singers to perform at different points in the service, but only two of them sang. Lawrence reflected, "I don't think I ever brought it up with John because when it was all said and done, it didn't really matter." And it was a good time, nonetheless.

Spurgeon and Menton

During their studies of Spurgeon, they learned the Prince of Preachers had suffered excruciating pain from gout for many years. For relief, he traveled to Menton, France. John and Lawrence made it their goal to go there together someday. In 2017, John was diagnosed with ALS, or Lou Gehrig's disease. When Lawrence talked with John on the phone after the diagnosis, he said, "It doesn't look like we're going to get to Menton." As Lawrence shared in the fall of 2019, and with unexpected emotion, John had replied that "he didn't want to go there without me." It was something they had talked about for at least thirty years. Such was their friendship as brothers in Christ.

Two months before John's death in January 2020, Lawrence visited John and Dawn. Lawrence assumed, given John's condition, that they would not be attending worship on the Lord's day. On the Sunday morning of his visit, Lawrence was up early and having a cup of coffee when he realized John and Dawn planned to attend the morning service. Not having brought church-clothes, Lawrence told Dawn he would just stay at home and see them when they returned. The story continued,

> She would have none of it. She said it didn't matter if I was dressed casually and that John would be disappointed if I did

> not attend. Consequently, I got ready and met them at church a little late. I did not know why it was so important to John that I attend until we sang the final hymn. It was *Amidst Us Our Beloved Stands* by C. H. Spurgeon, and John had requested that it be sung because he knew I would be there.[3]

Later, Lawrence shared his embarrassment that with all he had read by and about Spurgeon, he had been unaware that he wrote hymns. "That hymn will always be special to me," Lawrence said. It must have been special to John as well.

The pastor-theologian over whom they first bonded forty years earlier, Charles Spurgeon, had this to say of Psalm 134, which begins, "Behold, bless ye the LORD, all ye servants of the LORD, which by night stand in the house of the LORD":

> We have now reached the last of the Gradual Psalms. The Pilgrims are going home, and are singing the last song in their Psalter. They leave early in the morning, before the day has fully commenced, for the journey is long for many of them. While yet the night lingers they are on the move. As soon as they are outside the gates they see the guards upon the temple wall, and the lamps shining from the windows of the chambers which surround the sanctuary; therefore, moved by the sight, they chant a farewell to the perpetual attendants upon the holy shrine. Their parting exhortation arouses the priests to pronounce upon them a blessing out of the holy place. . . . The priests as good as say, "You have desired us to bless the Lord, and now we pray the Lord to bless you."[4]

At least since David and Jonathan's day (I Samuel 18 and following), godly male friendships have always been important. May our churches

3 E-mail, E. Lawrence Kersten to author, "Re: Hymns by Spurgeon," May 25, 2020.

4 Charles H. Spurgeon, *The Treasury of David . . . Volume Three, Psalm CXI to CL* (Hendrickson Publishers, Inc.: Peabody, Mass., 2008), 176.

learn to encourage our young men in the rising generation to pursue such friendships in the Christian faith as modeled by these two "Pilgrims [who] are going home"; indeed, to a better-than-Menton home.

[Note: A similar version of this chapter was published online by *The Aquila Report*, Nov. 26, 2019.]

6

SEMINARY AND DUSK-TO-DAWN ON *DELTA*

In the spring of 1982, John graduated from Fresno State University with a bachelor's degree in Communication. He planned on pursuing a seminary degree and then going into the ministry. Early on, John had considered following in his father's career path in the medical profession, but as John began to grow spiritually he became convinced that God was calling him to minister to the souls of men and women rather than to their bodies. When John shared his heart's desire, his dad was supportive. He told John, "You will never be rich, but you will have a meaningful life."

The International School of Theology, San Bernardino, California

In the fall of 1982, John began studies at the International School of Theology (ISOT) located not far from Los Angeles, in San Bernardino, California. One aspect of the school John found attractive was the Master of Divinity program requirement to be involved in field ministry as well as classroom studies. While they were students at Fresno State, the ambitious theological reading program that John and Lawrence Kersten shared had included Edith Schaeffer's book, *L'Abri* (shelter, in French). Each of them also read at least one of her husband Francis Schaeffer's many books, so John was well prepared for classroom discussions at ISOT on the ideas the Schaeffers had introduced him to.

Looking back from 2020, Dawn Geiger recalled that in the mid-1980s the L'Abri ministry, founded by the Schaeffers in Switzerland, had been her "doorway" to ISOT. Dawn grew up in Montgomery and after high school headed north to Vanderbilt University in Nashville, Tennessee, graduating in the spring of 1984. Her degree was in French, and that summer she had the opportunity to spend several months in France to continue learning the language and culture. Her parents joined her in France for part of that summer. In 1982, her only sibling, Michael, had died, and Dawn, although a Christian, was struggling in her relationship with God as a result. Understanding her hurt, her parents—who of course were suffering their own grief—encouraged her to spend time at L'Abri before returning home. Some have described L'Abri as part seminary, part commune, where visitors—including agnostics—were welcome to stay, help with chores, and discuss worldviews and theology. Dawn spent all of October and most of November there, during which time she was exposed to biblical truths she needed to hear. In particular, she found refreshing and immeasurably helpful the concept that God had not designed death in His created order, but, rather, death had entered the world because of human sin. As Romans 5:12 expresses, ". . . *through one man sin entered into the world, and death through sin, and so death spread to all men, because all sinned. . . .*"

Although she would have loved to stay longer at L'Abri, she returned home in time for Thanksgiving with her parents (her brother had died on Thanksgiving Day two years earlier). Not long after, Dawn received a brochure from ISOT advertising a L'Abri conference to be held early in 1985. Having just returned home from L'Abri, she did not attend. (John, in his third year at ISOT, attended that conference.) But for Dawn at that time, "any friend of L'Abri was a friend of mine," and she began looking seriously at the seminary's programs. The following summer, she attended an ISOT program in Colorado Springs, Colorado, after which she was convinced that the Southern California seminary was where she needed to be. Only later did Dawn appreciate the significance of her parents' support at that critical time in her life, including allowing her to go so far away—her father served on the board of a different seminary, which was also much closer to home.

By the fall, which was Dawn's first semester at the school, John was serving as a full-time youth pastor in Alta Loma as well as a full-time seminary student at ISOT. (This was John's second youth pastorate; he had devoted the 1979-1980 academic year to serving First Baptist, Visalia.) Alta Loma was considered a part of the city of Rancho Cucamonga near the foothills of the San Gabriel Mountains, and was fifteen or twenty miles from the seminary. During one of John's previous summers as a seminarian, he spent time in India with a cross-cultural ministry internship, and he devoted the summer of 1985 to working in Modesto, California (northern California), with a vocational internship. When he returned south to the Los Angeles area in the fall, he was invited to share his Modesto experience during an ISOT chapel program. Dawn was in the audience. She recalled that although John's allotted time was cut short by the long-winded speaker who preceded him, he was funny and all of his points began with the same letter of the alphabet. Later, she happened to pass by him as he relaxed with several other students and called out, "Hey, nice talk," to which John replied, "Thanks." It was the inauspicious start to their relationship. Unknown to Dawn at the time, John had already noticed her one day from across the area on campus known as "the Quad," and had been struck with the thought that he was to marry her. In 2018, when referring to the start of their relationship, John quipped, "God hadn't told *her*."

Not long after John's talk, Dawn spoke in chapel on her experience at L'Abri from the year prior. This time, John was in the audience. Later, John admitted he had experienced a strange sensation—he was certain he was listening to the words of his future wife. Toward the Thanksgiving break, John saw her in the library and asked her out for coffee, but Dawn's schedule was filled at the time. They agreed to try again later. Eventually (or so it seemed to John), he managed to get a lunch meeting with Dawn, which consisted of "garbage burritos" from Rosa Maria's—it was, technically speaking, their first date.

John graduated from seminary in the spring of 1986 and continued serving as the youth pastor at Community Baptist Church in Alta Loma. He had made his intentions clear from the start with Dawn and met her parents when they came out for spring break. At the end of her first year at ISOT, Dawn spent the summer in Eastern Europe as part of a ministry team working in a number of "closed countries"—recall the Iron Curtain was still in place and the Cold War lingered. Her team ministered in Poland, Hungary, Czechoslovakia, and the Soviet Union. John called it "The Summer of Silence" because, apparently, he never heard from Dawn while she was away. In her defense, she was busy. When she returned at the end of the summer, Dawn moved out to Alta Loma to help with the college ministry at John's church, Community Baptist. *(Any strings John may have pulled to get Dawn onto his ministry team remained undisclosed.)*

While their relationship deepened, Dawn had told John not to ask her to marry him "until you think I'm ready." By the fall of 1987, that time seemed near, except that Dawn was undergoing personality tests as a prerequisite for missionary team assignments. She was getting the message from some, perhaps even a professor, that someone with her personality traits shouldn't be paired with someone possessing John's traits. It gave her pause. Thankfully, a wise professor mentioned there was no perfect pattern for marriage, which was what she needed to hear. That Thanksgiving, she joined John and his large family in Visalia, California. Dorothy, John's mom, mistakenly thought they were officially engaged and had ordered a cake from town to be picked up several hours after their arrival. As the lively conversation continued and nothing was said about wedding plans, it dawned on her that they were not yet engaged. Dorothy called the cake shop and had them add another layer of icing to the prematurely lettered cake!

Dusk-to-Dawn on *Delta*, December 24/25, 1987

[Note: The below are John Geiger's own words as recorded on Sep. 8, 2018, at the Geiger home in Montgomery, Alabama. With permission of Dawn Geiger, minor edits to the actual words spoken have been made for ease of reading.]

"Now, by this time, she was no longer running from me, and I knew I *had* her, but I made her wait longer than she thought to propose. It was payback! I had planned on a Christmas Day proposal. Now, she had thought maybe the proposal would be on her birthday, no . . . maybe Thanksgiving, no. So I put her on a plane to go home for Christmas break. (We're grad students.) And I say, 'Goodbye, I'll see you in January.' And she said—with a look of uncertainty—'Okay.' I had planned on Christmas Eve to fly all night. So, the flight was at one o'clock in the morning, out of LAX, Los Angeles International. I drove around the airport. Every long-term parking lot was full, and I was new to flying across the country. I was using *Delta*, I had never used *Delta* before. And I thought, I'm going to miss my flight. I saw a building, a parking deck that said, '*Delta*.' I thought, whoa, they have their own parking deck for customers. (I'm 29 at this time.) So, I drove up and the man at the gate said, 'Do you have a pass?' I said, 'No, where do I get one?' He looked at me and said, 'Well, across the street at the office.' This is eleven-thirty at night. So, I said, 'I'll be right back.' I parked my car and went in, it was kind of a warehouse office, and there was a woman at the desk. I said, 'I need a parking pass.' And she gave me one. I turned and I walked back to the man, gave him my pass, parked my El Camino, grabbed my guitar and my suitcase and went back to the man at the gate. And I said, 'Where's the shuttle, how do I get to the airport?' (I'm a few miles away.) He said, 'Well, go back to the office, and keep going, and there's a shuttle.' [JG:] 'Oh, thank you.' So I walked back with my guitar and suitcase, and I see the lady at the desk, nod to her, and walked down the hall, through some double doors, and there's a bus right there. I load my stuff. (I just want to get to Montgomery.)"

"I get on the bus, and the bus driver said, 'What flight?' I tell him, 'Gate 69C.' And I get on and I see the men in overalls, a few stewardesses, a pilot or two. And I thought, I'll go with it. The bus starts driving, and now he's driving out on the runway and the tarmac. About this time I realized, *something* went wrong.

I thought, well, he was confident this will get me on the plane. I'm the last one he lets off. He pulls up right by the jet. They're loading luggage and fuel, and he lets me off, and points to my jet. I get off and I say, 'Merry Christmas.' I'm standing out there with the jet noise, my hair blowing, my guitar, and my bag . . . it's midnight. And I see a man with ear protectors working, and I ask him, 'How do I get on this jet?' He looked at me. I smiled. He said, 'Well, walk over there through that door, walk up the ramp, come to the elevator, punch in the security code, and the elevator will take you there.' I said, 'All right, Merry Christmas.' I start walking and realize everything's fine except that security code part of the plan. Well, as I'm walking, two other employees are walking to the ramp. I slow up, let them go first, and I'm right behind them with my guitar. They get to the elevator, punch in the code, we get on, they get off, first floor. I get off, second floor, open the door, and Burger King is right in front of me, and my gate is only a hundred feet away."

"I walk up to the gate (in those days you had paper tickets). I give it to him. He said, 'Well, you haven't checked in.' I said, 'You're right.' He looked at me and said, 'How'd you get those bags here? How did *you* get here?' So I had to tell him the story. He looked at me with incredulity. He said, '*Somebody's* in trouble. It's not you. But somebody. You broke security.' And this is before all the really bad stuff. So he made me go back and check in. I made it. I proposed with music. She said, 'Yes.' But on the flight over, I thought, 'Wow. How am I going to get back to my car? I can't go backwards.' I remembered a hotel nearby, as I was circling the airport parking area. So when I flew back from Montgomery, I took the shuttle to the hotel and walked across the street. There was my car, and I drove off. Problem solved!"

"In love. . . . It started out with no intention of breaking the law, just trying to figure out how to get from one place to another."

7

Marriage and Russia

After the excitement of the 1987 Christmas season, which included John and Dawn's engagement, John returned to youth ministry at Alta Loma and Dawn to seminary at San Bernardino. While Dawn didn't sense that she had neglected her studies in the spring of 1988—her final semester at the International School of Theology—her grades "said otherwise," she concluded. In any case, Dawn graduated in the spring and returned home to Alabama to prepare for the wedding, set for mid-August. On the thirteenth of August, John and Dawn were married at Capitol Heights Baptist in Montgomery—where her grandparents had been members from the church's earliest days—with John and Dawn's senior pastor from Alta Loma, Rev. Bob Logan, performing the ceremony. The reception, attended by four to five hundred family and friends, was held at the Nolins' picturesque home known affectionately as "the hill," near historic, downtown Montgomery. Only later did Dawn and John realize that for a family likely to be tied to a school calendar for many years, an August 13 wedding meant that, more often than not, they would celebrate their anniversary with hundreds of other peoples' kids as the fall term began.

Not long after the wedding, John and Dawn traveled to Europe, spending about three months visiting different ministries as well as sightseeing in Belgium, Poland, and Switzerland. Just after Christmas, they spent time at L'Abri. One small testament to how grateful Dawn was for L'Abri's ministry in her life was in the tablecloths that adorned the dining room tables she and John ate from when they stayed there. Four years earlier, Dawn had noticed the tablecloths were too short, so upon returning home, she and her mom gave longer ones to L'Abri. John and Dawn flew home from Europe in January of 1989. John had been in some form of youth ministry since 1978 and was ready for a change. Particularly, and not surprisingly, he found it challenging to take them "from fun and games to the Cross," as he expressed to Dawn during the transition.

Upon returning stateside, the newlyweds settled in Montgomery, residing in the Carriage House (or Guest House) on the grounds of "the hill." Andrew Nolin, Dawn's father, who grew up there from about the age of six, was active in various business enterprises. As a young man he had done everything from surveying to the U.S. Marine Corps and, later, from owning a commercial refrigeration company to "drilling holes in the ground hunting oil" out West. Some of his business dealings called for the use of a real estate agent. As John was not yet sure of his long-term plans, he decided to get his real estate license in order to assist his father-in-law. While John was certainly capable in real estate, it was not his passion. His father-in-law noted that in conversations he and John had with business partners whom Mr. Nolin had known for years, John quickly found out more about them than Andrew had ever known. People, not real estate, were John's passion. John also did handyman work for Andrew on some of the properties on "the hill," and for a time John ran his own lawn service. In 2019, Mr. Nolin commented that "John became a pretty good under-the-sink plumber and a pretty good carpenter also," but he never cared much for electricity.

If in 1988 John and Dawn had been able to peek into the future, they might have found it intriguing, if not also encouraging, that *six-decade marriages* seemed to be almost the norm in both of their families. John's parents, Robert and Dorothy Geiger, were married for 62 years; two of Robert's three siblings also were married for at least sixty years. As of this book's writing, Dawn's parents, Andrew and Syble Nolin, have been married 62 years; and Andrew's parents, "A.C." and Agnes Nolin, were married for at least sixty years. In God's kind providence, He was to bless John and Dawn with one-half of the time that many others in the family had been granted: 31 years.

In addition to working closely with his son-in-law during the early years of John and Dawn's marriage, Andrew observed John's cultural adjustment to life in the South. "He came out of California, so he didn't know anything about Southern food," Andrew said, "but he learned." As his father-in-law and others attested, John became a good cook of a number of Southern dishes. John had done plenty of hunting out West as a young man, but it was different in the South. For example, dove-hunts—which Andrew and John often joined in—typically involved one hundred or more birds flying over one area, far more than in many locales out West, Andrew noted. In yet another area in which John found himself culturally unprepared for life in Montgomery—more than a few might tout it as the no. 1 issue—when he first arrived and was asked if he was *for* Auburn or Alabama (football, obviously), he didn't know which one to choose. Regardless of such early challenges, John came to earn the highest praise any son-in-law could hope for: in 2019, Andrew and Syble agreed that "John has been more of a son to us than a son-in-law."

In July 1990, John and Dawn welcomed their first-born, Soren, into the family. The Nolins, of course, were pleased to have their grandson living only a few yards away from their home. Like many grandfathers—in later years, John became one of them—Andrew enjoyed his "four-wheeler" (in Andrew's case, an all-terrain vehicle) in which he could ride his grandson around the property.

One amusing evolution had to do with safety precautions for the kids. Andrew recalled the progression from Soren to Mary Agnes to Nolin, which went something like this: "I'd ride him on that four-wheeler, but they'd make me put a belt around both of us . . . the second one came along and they said, you hold onto 'em real tight . . . [by] the time Nolin came, it was kinda like, don't let him ride it by himself!"

Russia Ministry

The early 1990s were momentous times, especially in Europe, with the end of the Cold War and the Soviet Union's dissolution in 1991. (The

Berlin Wall came down in late 1989.) From their California days, John and Dawn enjoyed contacts with the ministry now known as Cru, led by Bill Bright. Late in 1991, through Cru, John began hearing of tremendous needs and ministry opportunities in what was becoming known (once again) as Russia. Given the breakup of the former Soviet republics and the crumbling of a police state, resulting in increased civil liberties, the Russian Ministry of Education realized there was a great need for moral and ethical instruction of the nation's youth—some thirty million of them. Russian educational leaders looked to Christian ministries in the West for help. At some point, Bill Bright had been in Russia showing the *Jesus* film, which was well received. When the education ministry asked if he could begin showing the film to all their schoolchildren as an inroad to teaching morality and ethics, Bright agreed to the massive undertaking even though it was well beyond his—or any other ministry's—resources. The ministries in the West would have to join forces to help the Russians. Eventually, about seventy ministries did so.

Late in the year, John spent a couple of days at a cabin on Lake Jordan, praying over whether or not to pursue these possibilities. When he returned, he had decided to travel to Russia for two weeks to see for himself what was happening. As things developed, John made two short trips to Russia early in 1992 (one of them with Dawn), then in May he flew over intending to spend a year with the "CoMission" ministry (which was supported by others including the Navigators, Youth for Christ, Youth with a Mission, Larry Burkett's Money Management, and Walk Through the Bible). Several weeks later, Dawn and Soren, accompanied by Syble, flew to Moscow. Dawn's mom stayed for several days, then flew home, while the Geigers settled into a friend's apartment for the first several months. In September, they moved into their own apartment in Moscow. John and Dawn considered it a privilege to serve in Russia during the period of post-Cold-War openness; it was a much different climate than Dawn experienced in 1986.

The Russians had committed to a five-year program in hopes of getting all their schoolchildren to see the film and to receive related instruction. Bill Bright agreed to provide counselors who could speak at teachers' conferences to be held at the level of the oblast (an administrative division), organized and carried out under the auspices of the Russian Ministry of Education. Typically, forty or fifty missionaries participated in a given conference, which featured a showing of the *Jesus* film, presentations by missionaries, and group discussions of the Christian worldview and the foundations of morality. The presentations were in English and the Russians provided the translators—many of whom, John said, came to faith in Christ.

Using the Bible and other sources, the Western missionary-counselors taught the Russian schoolteachers—typically, some three hundred per conference—about the life of Jesus Christ. The teachers then were to teach their own students, including the desired emphasis on morality and ethics. John became "the set-up man" for many of those conferences, which were held in various cities including Moscow, Petrozavodsk (northwest Russia, not far from Finland), and Volgograd (southwest Russia, and the site of the massive, brutal Battle of Stalingrad in 1942-1943). Interestingly, Petrozavodsk was the sister city of Burlington, Vermont, where Ben & Jerry's Ice Cream was founded in 1978. While in the Russian city, two-year-old Soren Geiger relished a Ben & Jerry's ice cream from the local shop which his parents captured on camera.

For many conferences that year, Dawn and Soren remained in Moscow while John traveled alone. It made for a frightening time for Dawn, as she sometimes had to accept rides with her toddler son on icy roads and with people she didn't know. Fuel prices rose. There were no seatbelts. It had not been that long since the 1986 nuclear disaster at Chernobyl on the Ukrainian-Belarus border, and the long-term effects of the radiation were still unclear even while nuclear plants were about to be restarted.

One city outside Russia they traveled to was Kiev, Ukraine, the capital of another of the newly-independent former Soviet republics. The Ukrainians were very interested in obtaining Bibles in Ukrainian, not Russian. Sometimes a truck mistakenly arrived with Bibles in Russian, and John had to do his best to straighten things out. There were no cell phones in those days. Later, Dawn recalled John had felt kind of "like it was all happening without him." John was there, but it was God doing the work, as many people, starved for the Word of God, finally had the chance to learn of Christ and the gospel by reading it for themselves.

John and Dawn forged friendships during that first year that continued over the long term. Gary and Luci Stanley, whom they knew from their seminary days, worked with them in Russia as part of the CoMission. For the next three decades, whenever the Stanleys were in Alabama they made a point to visit the Geigers, including just before John began hospice care. Another friend from their time in Russia was Steve Seibert who visited with John for the last time in October 2019. Steve offered to help John with basic tasks he could no longer do for himself—including making chicken soup—which John directed (via texting) to a tasty outcome. During Steve's drive home to Minnesota, he reflected on his time with John:

> I had always thought the Holy Spirit gives grace to do things and often gives joy when we do them. But I think the Lord showed me that it was really Jesus inside of me who wanted to serve John, and he used my hands and feet. And it wasn't so much the Holy Spirit giving me joy, but it was Jesus' joy that overflowed as he cared for [a son of His] that I was sensing. He is so much better and kinder than I can imagine![1]

From their days on the mission field to John's last days on earth, Dawn viewed such friends and others like them as examples of the proverb, "*A friend loves at all times, And a brother is born for adversity*" (Proverbs 17:17).

As the spring of 1993 advanced toward summer, Dawn was nearing the birth of their second child. By early June, the Geigers had returned home to Montgomery, Alabama, where in late July, they greeted their newborn daughter, Mary Agnes.

---

1 E-mail, Dawn N. Geiger to author, "Re: Chapter 7," Jul. 12, 2020. She had been in contact with Seibert who shared his thoughts.

8

Russia Again, and Songwriting

The Geigers were back in Montgomery by the summer of 1993, but John was not home for long. Within several months, he led a team from the United States to Russia whose members participated in one of the ongoing conferences arranged by the Russian education ministry. Typically, the trips—several each year during most of the 1990s—required John to be gone from home for about three weeks at a time.

Russia Again

Dawn recalled that another piece of the ministry kaleidoscope with a presence in the former Soviet republics was the Joni Eareckson Tada ministry known as Joni and Friends, a Christian outreach to the disabled community. The Russians wanted her ministry there, too.

John continued leading ministry teams overseas on a semi-regular basis, but in 1994 he and Dawn experienced a sort of Macedonian call (as recorded in Acts 16:9, the Apostle Paul saw a vision in the night: "*. . . a certain man of Macedonia was standing and appealing to him, and saying, 'Come over to Macedonia and help us.'*"). The

Russians were ready for the second phase of the CoMission conferences for their schoolteachers, who were then to pass along what they learned regarding the Christian worldview and Bible-based ethics and morality to their students.[1] As Dawn shared in 2020, the Russians specifically requested that John Geiger come over and manage the second phase for them.

John and Dawn—this time with two young children (Soren was 4 years old, and Mary Agnes 18 months)—left for Moscow at the start of 1995. To say that Dawn's parents were not happy at losing their grandchildren for another year—especially going to "the *Soviet Union*"—was a huge understatement. It was a tough decision for the whole family, but how could they refuse God's call?

The Geigers again rented an apartment in Moscow, this time from January 1995 to January 1996. While John was heavily involved in setting up the various conferences in cities all over Russia as well as Ukraine, he also came to realize that much of the work did not require him to be on-site. As a result, he felt his role was not as clear as it had been three years earlier when the conferences were a new thing.

Soren, John and Dawn's older son, remembered his time in Russia. During their first year in Moscow (1992-1993), two-year-old Soren's very first memory—*anywhere*—was of his dad making a "pillow-and-blanket fort" on the floor of their apartment. Crawling through the long, dark tunnel with unknown passageways was rewarded when, at the end of the ordeal, he discovered the television, covered by a blanket, where he and John proceeded to watch *Mary Poppins*. It was perhaps the most memorable of many improvised forts.

During the family's second year in Russia (1995-1996), Soren's most memorable experience—perhaps Dawn's as well (!)—was when he became separated from his mom in a sort of Russian *Costco*—a

---

1 The beloved Presbyterian and Reformed scholar-pastor, R. C. Sproul, distinguished ethics and morals in simple terms by saying, ethics is "*ought*-ness"; morality is "*is*-ness." Thus, for the Christian, ethics do not change because the Bible's moral law (summarized in the Ten Commandments) does not change; morality may change in a society, however, and it often does.

very large store that included outside vendors just beyond the doors. John was elsewhere at the time—he was often working with the conferences—so Dawn ended up leaving two-year-old Mary Agnes in the care of one of the Russian vendors and went back into the store alone so she could search more quickly. Within fifteen minutes she found five-year-old Soren, but it was a harrowing experience. Soren also remembered the great sledding that year during the snowy months.

In 2020, Soren, married and a father himself, recalled how John had made a serious effort to be as present as he could be in his children's lives. John traveled a lot in the 1990s when both Soren and Mary Agnes were very young, and he often recorded stories and songs that Dawn could let them listen to when he was away. The kids heard their father's voice even when he was away from them, a theme with a strong scriptural basis, as in the closing lines of Psalm 91 where the believer hears the very words of his Father: *"He will call upon Me, and I will answer him; I will be with him in trouble; I will rescue him, and honor him."* The psalmist, perhaps Moses, continues, *"With a long life I will satisfy him, And let him behold My salvation."* Spurgeon, whose writings John loved, commented on this section of the psalm, "Here we have the Lord himself speaking of his own chosen one." Addressing verse 15, Spurgeon wrote: "The man described in this Psalm fills out the measure of his days, and whether he dies young or old he is quite satisfied with life, and is content to leave it. He shall rise from life's banquet as a man who has had enough, and would not have more even if he could."[2]

One of the men John befriended during his family's second year in Russia was a businessman who did well in the post-1991, more-or-less-capitalist economy. While the realities of Russian politics, especially under Vladimir Putin's authoritarian rule some years later, precluded using the man's name in social, and printed, media—including the present work—he and John remained friends. In 2018,

2 Charles H. Spurgeon, *The Treasury of David . . . Volume Two, Psalm LVIII to CX* (Hendrickson Publishers, Inc.: Peabody, Mass., 2008), 94.

when John traveled to Europe for the last time, he and Nolin spent several days relaxing with him and his family at their home in Barcelona, Spain. During their time together, John continued ministering from the Scriptures to his Russian friend and Christian brother with whom he had first shared the gospel a quarter-century earlier (see Chapter 17).

John's Songwriting

When the family came home to Montgomery at the start of 1996, Soren was five, Mary Agnes only two-and-a-half. John loved music and wrote dozens of his own songs. The early years of John and Dawn's children were some of John's more productive years in terms of his songwriting. By 2020, Mary Agnes was married and the mother of two little girls. She shared memories of her dad's music, saying, "It's a really wonderful thing to be able to associate so much fun music with Dad." Eric—her husband and fellow Hillsdale College grad—and Mary Agnes's two-year-old daughter, Evelyn, walks around the house singing John's "playground song . . . and *she's two*" (see Appendix A).

Many others have appreciated John's songs written for young children, including Lynn Grace, the secretary of Eastwood Presbyterian. She recalled the first time she really met John, during her first Vacation Bible School at Eastwood after moving to Montgomery. Lynn was helping with the 3- and 4-year-old class and John came in every day with his guitar to sing to the kids. She continued:

> Thinking back, one song in particular stands out. It was The Fruit of the Spirit song. Amazingly, by the end of the week, John had tricked the kids into learning the fruit of the Spirit without them even knowing. I later found out that John had actually been the one who had written the song.
>
> 'Love, joy, peace, these are fruits, they have no earthly branch or roots. The Spirit of God, He gives us all His good fruit. . . . Patience, kindness, goodness, these are fruits, they have no earthly branch or roots. The Spirit of God, He gives us all His good fruit. . . . Faithfulness, gentleness, self-control, these are

fruits, they have no earthly branch or roots. The Spirit of God, He gives us all His good fruit.'[3]

At the start of 1996, John, Dawn, Soren, and Mary Agnes returned home to Montgomery. John continued supporting the ministry conferences and he still traveled on the roughly three-week-long trips to Russia and Ukraine, but he also did much of the coordination from home. Within months, however, the start-up of a classical Christian school in his adopted hometown of Montgomery had caught his attention.

3 E-mail, Lynn Grace to author, "John's song," Jun. 19, 2020.

9

John and ECS, 1996 to 2003

In 1995, several Eastwood church families—notably, members Priscilla Stewart and Beth Beno—petitioned the church's elders (collectively known as the session) to consider starting a classical Christian school. The session approved the request, agreeing that such a school was to be considered an outreach ministry of the church as well as an option for the church's families. A school board was selected, consisting of elders and members. The session was to oversee the board and, thus, indirectly, the school. In 1992, Bob Maruna—a southern California native, a West Pointer (Class of 1983), and for nine years a U.S. Army aviator—had been hired as Eastwood church's administrator. Bob was to double as the new school's administrator (in later years he also taught and served as the upper school principal).

Bob recalled John Geiger expressed interest in the school very early, although for its first year he was committed to the ongoing CoMission ministry and was unavailable to teach. In fact, by 1996—Soren coming of school age was part of the equation—John was considering both *local* ministry (in Montgomery) and *school* ministry (classical Christian). He had been convicted by the Lord that he needed to be willing to reach out to his own community, not only overseas; and he was reading classical Christian educational materials.

By that time, John was working mainly from Montgomery in support of CoMission's ministry in Russia as well as, increasingly, Ukraine. He continued to travel overseas several times a year to manage the conferences, especially in Kiev but in other cities in Ukraine, too. By about 1996-1997, a big part of the reason for focusing on Ukraine was that in Russia, the Orthodox Church had begun clamping down on foreigners, "but Ukraine was very open," John said.

Fathering Ministry

With the opening up of Russia, Ukraine, and other Eastern European countries to the CoMission ministries in the early 1990s, other Christian groups also became involved in countries that had been behind the Iron Curtain. Among them was the National Center for Fathering, based in Kansas City, although it was 1997-1998 before they did so. By that time, the clamp-down in Russia combined with the openness in Ukraine created an excellent opportunity for a fathering-based work in the latter country. Under the by-then-defunct Soviet system, considerable state control over so much of the people's lives—plus the dearth of biblical teaching coupled with social ills such as alcohol abuse—had severely hindered the traditional role of fathers in the home.

John was introduced to the fathering ministry by someone with Bill Bright's ministry, and he was a natural fit for such work in Ukraine. The Ukrainians were trying to become more independent from Moscow, John said, and "they wanted to be different than the old Soviet man, who was drunk and controlled by his wife." In about 1998—by then he was teaching at Eastwood Christian School (ECS)—John began working with the National Center for Fathering as the international director, in which capacity he mainly planned and networked, but also traveled.

John was committed to providing resources for Ukrainian men who were asking for more information about their new roles as fathers in their fledgling democracy. As Ken Canfield, founder of the National Center for Fathering and author of *The 7 Secrets of Effective Fathers: Becoming the Father Your Children Need*, once said, "Fathering is a marathon—a long and often trying journey—and we must be disciplined if we hope to finish successfully."[1]

In 2020, Steve Wilson, who had co-labored with John in the center's ministry, recalled that "the work in Ukraine was the most fruitful. John joined and provided some leadership to a team that began making semi-annual trips to Ukraine in 1999" (John traveled in 1999 but by the next year conducted all his planning and networking from home). Steve noted that John's "heart for the Father and the fathers of Ukraine was evident, reflecting a foundational verse for the ministry, Malachi 4:6, '*He will turn the hearts of the fathers to their children and the hearts of the children to their fathers.*' "

Steve wrote that they "implemented a strategy to engage and train the fathers of Ukraine using conference formats and small group materials translated from [the center's] catalogue." Besides the capital of Kiev, other Ukrainian cities the team visited on a major trip in 1999 were Kharkiv, Simferopol, and Yalta. The team also connected with ministries in Vienna, Austria, and Bratislava, Slovakia. Overall, they spent time with ten denominations representing some two thousand churches, and conducted seven fathering conferences and workshops, in which three hundred men were trained to use the center's small group materials. Team members also spoke at universities, churches, and private groups totaling more than one thousand eight hundred attendees.

Among the Ukrainian pastors the team worked alongside was Oleksandr (Sasha) Marchenko, who was called to be the in-country leader of the fathering ministry. When interviewed in 2018, John had just received an e-mail from Pastor Marchenko, whom he had gotten to know in the fathering ministry twenty years earlier. More than twenty thousand men had received fathering instruction in those two decades. The work continues today organized as the International Center for Fathering.

Eastwood Christian School

It was probably in the spring of 1996 when Dawn noticed a small advertisement in a local publication about a new school starting up based on

1 "Fathering is a Marathon," *crosswalk.com*, Sep. 6, 2004, at https://www.crosswalk.com/family/parenting/fathering-is-a-marathon-1280864.html.

the classical Christian model, which she brought to her husband's attention. At least one ECS board member recalled John offering to teach as a volunteer—unpaid—when he became available. In later years, at least one teacher likened his initial teaching salary at ECS as not much higher than unpaid volunteer work. John, too, had worked for "pennies" in his early years as a teacher.

Teachers' salaries notwithstanding, classes began in the fall of 1996. There were eight upper school students that year, among them a husky ninth-grader, Bruce Stewart, who four years later became the first ECS graduate. In 1997, John began teaching humanities courses (including Bible) at the fledgling institution. There were only two full-time upper school teachers in those days: Denise Brassell—the first, beginning in 1996—who taught sciences and math, and John. Officially, they were part-time teachers: classes ended for the day at 12:30pm. But, probably for both Denise and John, keeping up with all their classes (and without a planning period in the morning) required a full-time effort and more than a few late nights.

In 2018, John, while dealing with what he termed "The Mucus Monster," hacking, and struggling mightily to speak, mused of 1997: "My heart was beginning to see the potential of school ministry, being with these kids thirty hours a week . . . meeting with dads and moms," and presenting a Christian worldview in all subjects. Bob Maruna remembered that for a time (perhaps in a later year) John taught *seven* different subjects including history, rhetoric, and theology/Bible. After beginning to teach, John continued to travel overseas, mainly to Ukraine. When he traveled during the school year, other teachers covered his absences for him until about the end of 1999 when he ceased to travel with the fathering ministry.

Regardless of the teaching load, it did not take long for John to realize that his ministry at ECS was God's calling on his life. That was despite certain students turning "Sweet Mr. Geiger" into "a Human Sundae," which they did on more than one ECS field day. Whether the term "sweet" referred to John's attitude about the whole thing or to the stuff poured on his head by the students was unclear!

The Headmaster of ECS

In the school's first year, 1996-1997, Vivian Arnold, an Eastwood church member with a strong background as a missionary teacher, had served as the ECS principal. There was no "headmaster" at that early point; there was no need with less than forty students that year. As the student population increased, the need for a headmaster became apparent, and, for the two academic years beginning in the fall of 1998, Rev. Henry Beaulieu, an Eastwood pastor, served as headmaster. From the fall of 2000 until January 2002, Bob Maruna filled the headmaster billet (Bob was, in effect, headmaster-administrator). However, both Henry and Bob had other jobs outside the school (Henry also served part-time as a chaplain in the Alabama National Guard and, like Bob, was a former Army aviator). ECS had no full-time headmaster with long-term prospects, but it was starting to look for one.

In the fall of 2001, the Marunas—Bob, his wife Tomi, and their three children—lived in a small house on the grounds of "the hill," where Dawn had grown up. (Her parents, Andrew and Syble Nolin, lived in the house next door to John and Dawn's home, which allowed for plenty of grandparenting time; Dawn's grandparents had purchased "the hill" in 1944.) Someone suggested John's name to Bob as a candidate for headmaster (John was his landlord at the time). Sure enough, John was interested, and in January 2002 he began as ECS headmaster—the role in which he flourished for the next sixteen and a half years. In 2018, John recalled that a low-key welcoming reception had been planned—but nobody showed up, not one person. It was probably *so* low-key that the details were not properly disseminated, but in any case the contrast between that *non*-reception and the event held sixteen years later dubbed "A Knight to Celebrate"—honoring John as he neared retirement—was striking (see Chapter 15).

From the early days, ECS promoted a vision for ministering to needs outside their own walls. As John assumed his new role, in the spring of 2002 the fourth grade class ministered to an ailing Montgomery resident, Brad Christian. Brad suffered from ALS, or Lou Gehrig's disease. From the start of the year the children had prayed for him regularly, sent him homemade cards and letters, and at the end of the year visited him. A decade and a half later, another generation of ECS students ministered to their own beloved headmaster in like manner.

In 2001-2002, and for some years thereafter, the school did not have a designated upper school "principal." With John's elevation to headmaster, Rev. Vic Minish, who shared the humanities teaching load for several years with John, became the director of humanities in the upper school, in which role he continued until 2003. A favorite of many ECS students over her two decades of teaching, Denise Brassell served as the director of mathematics and sciences in the upper school, and, from 2003 to 2011, as the upper school director.[2] In 2002, Denise offered her thoughts on teaching those subjects:

> Teaching mathematics and science from a classical methodology provides the impetus . . . to discuss the majestic greatness of our God and Father, the Creator of all things. Through mathematics and science we delve into His unchanging nature and character. We . . . conclude that our existence is an orderly and amazing one. Within God lies everything (all knowledge) that we, as humans, seek to determine on our own. In His grace and mercy, he bestows upon both Christian and pagan the ability to ascertain qualities about Himself. While the pagan might not understand that the discovered information leads us back to the Almighty, we as believers can more clearly see God's role in our life's existence.[3]

Shifting into several specific examples, Denise observed, "From uniquely designed left-handed amino acids to downward hydrogen pointing bonds of the digestive system, all of these give evidence that life

2 Eastwood Christian School and its board considered a "principal" to be responsible for student discipline, but the designation of "director" did not imply that obligation. In order to spare Denise Brassell, a gifted female teacher, the burden of having to discipline upper school students, she was designated the upper school "director." The upper school did not have a "principal" until the fall of 2011.

3 [yearbook, compiled by Jessica Jones], *Eastwood Christian School 2002,* 31.

did not evolve or happen by mere random chance. It was with architectural precision and skill that God brought forth man made in His image."

Recollection: Benjamin "Allen" McDaniel, Class of 2003

There were no graduates in the spring of 2002, so John's first opportunity as headmaster to engage with ECS *seniors* was in the 2002-2003 academic year. Benjamin "Allen" McDaniel was one of four graduating seniors in 2003. Like many, if not most, ECS students in the early years, Allen had been homeschooled through the sixth grade and started at ECS in its second year as a seventh grader. He recalled being in John Geiger's Old Testament course that year. The fall of 1997 was also John's first semester of teaching at Eastwood. Two decades later, as Allen shared his recollections of John, Allen realized that his very first Old Testament class period of that fall—it was an eight o'clock class, the first of the day—probably was the *first hour* of John Geiger's teaching career at the school.

Allen—who upon graduation from ECS attended Auburn University, earning a pharmacy doctorate in 2010—remembered John's informal, effective teaching style, much more roundtable discussion than lecture. One especially memorable event was when John, who opened each day's "homeroom" time with prayer, began with, "Good Morning, Dad...." As John probably intended, at least one of his students that day was impressed enough to realize, perhaps some time later, that the Christian enjoys the high privilege of coming to God as his "Abba, Father," as the Apostle Paul writes in Romans.[4] Allen also came to appreciate his gifted teacher's calm and patient assistance as he prepared his graduation speech, John coaching him in such areas as voice inflection, eye contact, and more. Just perhaps, Allen's selection of his speech's theme—the famous Trojan War horse—reflected as much John's passions as his own. In any case, Allen's first public speaking opportunity to a large crowd, on graduation night, was a well-earned success.

---

4 As with other spiritual privileges, intimacy with the Lord in prayer is to be held in tension with a due reverence for God.

Procrastination and Peach Cobbler

While John had occasion to *get onto* his students to accomplish their assignments on time, the ladies in the ECS front office confessed that sometimes their headmaster needed the same treatment to get his yearbook comments turned in. One of them mentioned their boss's confession, when with a smile he said, "I know I'm a procrastinator, but I don't like other people to be." Whether he had required any special prodding or not, John's comments for the 2002-2003 yearbook were "classic John Geiger," as some have used the phrase. He began:

> We had peach cobbler the other day. It ranks on my "all-time-favorite-dessert" list. What made it particularly tasty was that the cobbler began about five years ago. The sapling was planted by our hands, fertilized straight from my daughter's horse, and protected from the savage squirrels. We waited. Over time edible fruit developed . . . and we developed it into an edible cobbler.[5]

Following his introduction, John reminded readers that the Apostle Paul exhorts us not to "'become weary in doing good, for at the proper time we will reap a harvest if we do not give up,'" and that ECS "seeks to share the load with you." One of those who had borne that load was Sandy Wallace, a favorite teacher and the principal of the lower school, who departed ECS at the close of the school year in 2003. She liked to think of the 165 children of the lower school as "'my' children," and in her parting words to them shared from 3 John, verse 4: "I have no greater joy than to hear that my children are walking in the truth."

Sheila Graves: Children's Director and ECS Teacher

The experience of an Eastwood church member and ECS teacher, Sheila Graves, illustrated well the overlapping of church and school life for many in those years and at the same time a long-term friendship with

5 [yearbook] *Eastwood [Christian School] 2002-2003*, 3.

John and Dawn Geiger. Starting in 1994, Sheila served fifteen years as the Eastwood children's director of Christian education and in that capacity was responsible for planning and running the children's version of the annual Eastwood missions conference. She also taught geography in the upper school beginning in 2002. For most of those years, Sheila recalled that John and Dawn were her primary assistants with the children's conference, which typically involved three events, held on Thursday and Friday nights and one on Saturday.

The three of them wrote their own curriculum and came up with all the songs, crafts, and activities for the children, which were aimed at reinforcing the theme of Eastwood's conference each spring. About a week prior, the Geigers' hosted a dinner at their home featuring a meal from one of the countries to be represented at the conference. Sheila, John, and Dawn reviewed the entire children's program, taking care of everything from making the nametags for perhaps two hundred fifty children, to ensuring realistic costumes and room decorations were ready, to practicing their lines and songs, to reviewing the logistical plan for providing snacks and drinks for the kids.

One of the most memorable conferences employed the theme of "the Persecuted Church." That year, 2003, Sheila and the Geigers turned an unfinished and unused stairwell in the Eastwood church building into a "prison." The Geigers' older son, Soren, was of course delighted to dress up and play the part of a mean prison guard. During the conference, groups of children were "arrested" at different times for having attended an underground church service. They perhaps gleaned a tiny glimpse of the persecution many believers in Christ have endured throughout church history to the present day.

10

John and ECS, 2003 to 2008

Through the spring of 2005, ECS did not have more than four graduates in a given year. Beginning in 2004, however, and for the next several years, Eastwood homeschool seniors participated in joint graduations with their ECS counterparts. The first homeschool graduate to do so, Samantha Gamble, took John's rhetoric course along with the four ECS seniors and so also benefited from his public speaking expertise.

Recollection: Beth McDaniel, Class of 2005

One of the four ECS graduates in 2005, Beth McDaniel, expressed her view—one widely shared—that "there was no better expert in public speaking than John Geiger." He engaged the seniors, she recalled, in a kind, encouraging manner as he helped them prepare their graduation speeches. Most high school seniors, Beth included, were anxious (to put it lightly) at the prospect of addressing a crowd of adults, ECS peers, and younger students on graduation night. And "if you needed to practice five more times" as the big day approached, "he was ready to do that," she said. Beth chose the theme of her speech on the meaning of an education: "Education is not filling a bucket, but lighting a fire"[1]—as a lifelong learner. As part of the night's ceremony, Rev. Aaron Fleming, Eastwood's founding pastor—whose devoted service to the church spanned more than thirty years—charged the four graduates to live as servants of Jesus Christ.

Heeding her own exhortation, like her older brother (Benjamin "Allen") who graduated two years earlier from ECS, Beth kept up a rigorous family tradition and spent the next seven years at Auburn, earning a pharmacy doctorate. Both of their parents, Allen and Linda, are pharmacists and Auburn grads. They met in physiology class in 1978 when the instructor paired the students with lab partners in alphabetical order, and, in their class "McDaniel" immediately preceded "McFarland," Linda's surname. Interestingly, Linda had an uncle, "Johnny Mac" McFarland who spent many years in Alaska in the crabbing business and for a time skippered his own boat. His boat, as well as Bruce Geiger's (*Sirius*), was based out of tiny Homer in 1979 (population two thousand), so it was likely they had met, perhaps even at the Salty Dawg Saloon, a local hangout. If so, it was another fascinating *small world* illustration—or God's providence by another name: John's brother and the uncle of the wife of the longtime chairman of John's school board, having crabbed together in Alaska three decades earlier!

The McDaniel family tradition definitely included Auburn football. Beth attended almost all the home football games during her seven years there, including every home game in 2010 when the Cam Newton-led Tigers went undefeated (14-0) and won the BCS National Championship.[2]

Like many ECS students over the years, Beth recalled how invested John was in the students. "You always knew he had your best interests at heart," she said, and everyone felt how deeply he cared about them. In 2020, she added that her headmaster's little eccentricities had only

1 The quote is often misattributed to W. B. Yeats, but it seems likely to be a paraphrase of Plutarch; see Robert Strong, "'Education is not the filling of a pail, but the lighting of a fire': It's an inspiring quote, but did WB Yeats say it?" *The Irish Times*, Oct. 15, 2013.

2 BCS is "Bowl Championship Series."

made him more lovable. One small example was how "tickled" he was, typically, to see Beth and her inseparable classmate, Brittany Powers, together as friends. Another was John's practice at school assemblies to lead in prayer with, "Good Morning, Lord. . . ." "He talked to God as though He was in the room with us," Beth remembered. While she and her brother, Allen, had never discussed it together, John's practice of a genuine *intimacy in prayer* in front of his students had impressed and stayed with both of them for at least fifteen years. Most likely, they were not alone.

Recollection: Greg Teal, Class of 2005

Another 2005 graduate was Greg Teal, whose Air Force family had moved to Montgomery in 2001. Greg entered the tenth grade at ECS in 2002. Like a number of ECS graduates, Greg had strong recollections of Mr. Geiger's working with him on his senior speech in the required Rhetoric course. John coached them: You must have *desire*. "You have to *feel* it. If you are up there emotionless or passionless, people won't really care about what you're saying." He talked about the difference between *ethos* and *pathos*, Greg added.

Prior to graduation, Greg had the opportunity to do some student-teaching under David Givens, one of his instructors. It was enough to plant a seed. After ECS, Greg attended Auburn University and finished a bachelor's degree in history in three years. Sometime around 2006, he returned to ECS to participate in a parent-teacher event. Following the event, Mr. Geiger wrote him a brief note with something like, "Finish your B.A., come back and teach for me." In the spring of 2008, he interviewed for a history teaching position at Eastwood, talking with John and ECS board member Allen McDaniel (one of the few years when he was *not* the chairman). Greg was hired, and in the process became the first ECS alumnus to return as a teacher. Over the following decade, Greg had the opportunity to teach John and Dawn's second and third children, Mary Agnes and Nolin. He got to know Nolin well—having him in courses for five of his six years in the upper school—thus lending credibility to Greg's assessment of John as "a grown-up Nolin" in terms of his love for all things *warrior*!

The next year, 2005-2006, marked ten years for Eastwood Christian School. By the close of the school year there were nearly two hundred fifty students. While the lower school's classrooms remained on the ground floor of Eastwood church's facilities, a newly built, two-story education building opened in the spring of 2006 for the upper school's use. It was a major step up from the trailers behind the church building that had served an increasing number of upper school students for what seemed like forever.

Recollection: Hannah Crisler, Class of 2006

In the spring of 2006, Hannah Crisler was the only young woman among five ECS graduating seniors. Only during her senior year did she have Mr. Geiger as her teacher, during the fall for a required course, "The History of Thought," and in the spring for Rhetoric (also for a semester of British Literature).[3] The former was the more memorable of the two for Hannah, and she both enjoyed and benefited from the discussions she and her fellow seniors held with their teacher as they watched movies in his office and analyzed the worldviews depicted in them. But aside from those two courses, most of her interactions with John took place in the school office, where her mother, Joan Ellis, worked as office manager. Spending so much time over the years hanging around the school office (mostly doing homework) after classes were done for the day—because her mom was still working in the office—probably contributed to Hannah's intent, by the time she graduated, to rule out any consideration of teaching as a career.

After Eastwood, Hannah attended Erskine College in Due West, South Carolina, and graduated in 2010 with a double major in History and English. By the spring of 2011, she was back in Montgomery. Over the summer, Hannah considered doing some substitute teaching at ECS in the upcoming school year, but things changed quickly and by August she found herself teaching first-year Latin to ECS 7th graders. Hannah became the second ECS graduate to return to teach at Eastwood,

3 History of Thought was one of several courses that were taught, in some years, to 11th graders, in other years, to 12th graders.

where—nine years later as of this writing—she continues teaching mainly honors courses in American Literature and Medieval Literature and Latin. Once again, Proverbs 16:9 had come into play: "*The mind of man plans his way, But the LORD directs his steps.*"

Dawn Geiger: French Teacher

In 1984 Dawn had graduated from Vanderbilt University with a bachelor's degree in French and then spent time in France to improve her fluency. Twenty-two years later, she began using her French at ECS. As Dawn shared in 2015 as part of her testimony, when John hired her to teach French One, "His father-in-law rejoiced. Up to that moment I had recouped . . . well . . . $0 of my Vanderbilt BA in French . . . so good ole Dad was delighted to see me actually get a job with my stellar education even if it was my husband who hired me." She added, "I love teaching," which became evident to many ECS students in the years to come. One of her students for her first two years of teaching was Soren Geiger.

Cynthia Jones: ECS Office Manager

Shortly before the close of the school year in spring 2006, a local Christian teacher—open to God's leading her to someplace new—sent an e-mail to Katy Leach, the ECS lower school principal. Years later, Cynthia Jones confessed that she really didn't know *why* she had e-mailed her friend Katy, other than the name "Eastwood" had been whispered in her ear. Katy invited Cynthia to visit the school. Doing so, Cynthia told her, oddly, "I do not know *why* I'm here." Katy told her there was an opening to teach 2nd grade in the fall, but there was another impending move as well. Joan Ellis, the ECS office manager, was leaving soon because her husband, Frank, was to begin seminary in Missouri.

Persuaded that she should apply for the office manager job, Cynthia interviewed initially with John Geiger. She had never even heard his name prior to being told of the interview. During their time together, Cynthia could tell he was a little nervous, as was she. Clearing the first hurdle, she then met with ECS board members Glenn Draper and Scott

Pritchett. When Glenn offered her the job, Cynthia basically tried to talk him out of it, feeling herself inadequate for a position she had never done before. Thankfully, wise counsel prevailed, along with the help of a book she had been reading that encouraged "getting out of the boat" in the manner of a disciple of Jesus Christ. Cynthia took the job and started in June 2006.

Her office was next to John Geiger's. It took a few weeks, Cynthia recalled, but she got John to smile, and that broke the ice. After that they got along very well. She'd tease him at least once a week with something like, "I'm going to tell you this, but I know you're going to fire me." Staff meetings were light-hearted gatherings. John usually began them with a devotional or something he was thinking about. He liked "his white board," and used it to sketch out his evolving ideas for the school. Some of his gifts, she was convinced, included being a visionary and seeing the big picture, meeting with people, and sharing the gospel. Cynthia was far from the only ECS adult or parent to be impressed with John's ability, as she put it, to turn "a normal everyday conversation into a spiritual conversation and sharing the gospel with people on the spot and pretty quickly."

"He generated activity," Cynthia observed, but at times that made it hard for her to accomplish her primary duties in the office. While it perhaps did not require much time, one of the non-traditional activities John generated for her was to assist him with putting on his Zeus outfit for the lower school's annual Olympic Field Day. John's typical attire was a toga with a laurel wreath on his head (which Cynthia helped to adjust). The students carried Zeus on a sort of human chariot to open the games.

For the younger children, John always taught "the kindergarten song" and played it on his guitar, and he also played a piece for "the marriage of Q and U"—who faithfully remained wedded throughout the English language. For the third graders, John—in the garb and role of a rabbi—officiated over a Sader, the traditional Jewish meal at the time of Passover. And on a regular if not almost daily basis, John and Cynthia went outside for the morning carpool to greet the lower school children as they arrived. In the fall of 2014, seeing John warmly greeting the youngest schoolchildren as they arrived in the morning was the first impression of ECS—and a lasting one—for Seongho Choi, the Eastwood Presbyterian Church choir director.

While Cynthia enjoyed a perfect vantage point to see her boss's interactions with others on a daily basis, she especially appreciated the wisdom she gleaned from him. In the front office, Cynthia didn't interact much with the teachers, but she listened all the time to John's godly counsel with students and parents who came in to see him. In short, while maintaining her respect for John's authority—especially when there were tough decisions to be made—in 2019, she summed up their relationship: "He was a boss, he was a friend, he was a counselor."

Denise Brassell: Outstanding American Teacher Recognition

In 2006-2007, the school population continued to climb, with 264 students and 30 faculty members. A new playground added that year benefited the large number of lower school students as well as Eastwood's church families. The longest-serving ECS upper school teacher—and the upper school director, Denise Brassell—was inducted into the National Honor Roll's Outstanding American Teachers. The honor roll recognized educators "who have been identified by their students as having had the greatest influence on their lives, either as a student or as an individual." Perhaps part of Denise's ability to connect with her students was suggested the year prior when she performed as one of the four "Trailer Park" singers at the ECS back-to-school barbecue!

First Senior Class Trip to Europe, 2008

John had long sought to provide his students the opportunity "to see, and touch, and smell history." In the spring of 2008, John and Dawn led five ECS seniors, including their older son, Soren, on an unforgettable two-week journey to Europe. According to the 2008 yearbook, the senior trip, which included a missions emphasis, "traced the ideas that produced Western Civilization to their European roots." The adventure began in Rome, "where the ideas of ancient Greece, Christianity, and the Renaissance can be seen in amazing clarity and contrast." (According to

Soren, Rome was the favorite city of the ECS seniors.) Next, they traveled to Marseilles and Aix-en-Provence, France, where they met with missionaries and seminary students, respectively; and "ate couscous and discussed the spiritual climate of France and the history of the Huguenots." In Paris they spent time with a church-planter, Rev. David Lohnes and his wife, Kathryn, who were (and remain, in 2020) long-time Eastwood church members. David led the ECS group on a tour of the Normandy beaches of June 6th, 1944. In the fall of 2018, David did much the same with John and his brothers on their bittersweet Band of Brothers' tour, their last time together (see Chapter 16).

They proceeded to the Swiss Alps, where they experienced perhaps the most majestic view and memorable moment of the trip—seeing the French Alps, after taking an off-season ski gondola to a mountaintop on the Swiss side of the border. The late Dr. Francis Schaeffer's son-in-law, Udo Middelmann, showed them Reformation sites in Switzerland. In Basel, they visited Ellis Potter, formerly a colleague of Schaeffer and a friend of John and Dawn from their time at L'Abri twenty years earlier, and they enjoyed discussing topics from "the Beatles to Buddhism to the validity of the typical Christian testimony." From there they traveled to Germany, linking up with Rev. Stephen Spanjer, a former Eastwood church pastoral intern who was planting a church in southwest Germany's Black Forest region. On their final day, Stephen took them to a former concentration camp, which "stood in solemn contrast to the beauty of the Alps and the majesty of the cathedrals and castles" they had seen so recently.

The travelers summarized their amazing experience in the 2008 yearbook by paraphrasing Francis Schaeffer:

> Reality is like a keyhole and Christianity is the only key that fits. Ours is not a private faith as the French believe, nor a relic like the ones we saw in Italy. Our faith explains man's capacity for gross evil and his incomprehensible ability to achieve great beauty. The God who is there has spoken; His idea for mankind was sealed at the resurrection, and we must structure our lives to reflect that truth. A watching world wants to know if these ideas

> we espouse have consequences, and our lives must cry out with a resounding "Yes."[4]

With the exception of 2010 and 2014 when there were not enough seniors to go, for the following decade John and (except for two years) Dawn led a group of ECS seniors to Europe for what was a memorable, capstone experience to their classical Christian education.[5]

---

4 [yearbook] *Eastwood Warriors, 2007-2008*, 49.

5 In a 2018 interview, John noted that the first trip in 2008 had been too full. Later trips included fewer cities on the itinerary.

11

John and ECS, 2008 to 2012

As the 2008-2009 school year commenced, two major transitions had occurred in the ECS lower school. Katy Leach—for four years the lower school principal—returned to teaching. In her parting words, Katy shared that while enjoying her time as lower school principal, "I still had the heart of a teacher." John found a teaching spot for her with the 2nd graders. Meanwhile, Susan Gaines began as the lower school principal. Susan had taught at ECS for seven years; for the last six years, she and Marion Steindorff had shared the 3rd grade teaching load.

Susan Gaines: Lower School Principal

Susan and her husband, John, a Baptist pastor, had moved to Montgomery from LaFayette, Alabama, in 1998. The Gaines' two boys, Austin and Collin, began in the lower school in the fall of 1999, at which point Priscilla Stewart approached Susan about teaching in the lower school. Two years later, as Susan recalled, "The Lord's leadership and Priscilla's power of persuasion" finally convinced her to accept the 3rd grade teaching position in the fall of 2001.

In 2019, Susan shared that eleven years earlier she had not wanted to become the lower school principal. But because she knew the man she was to work for, she was okay with it. As a young woman, Susan had learned a lot from her father and so was very perceptive of John's role as headmaster. Even though Susan and John had related to each other for years at ECS, but not closely, she sensed, initially, that he wasn't sure he could trust her as he needed to. She perceived John as a cautious person in some ways, but also perhaps the most positive person she had ever known. Not wanting to walk on egg-shells in their relationship, Susan resolved to practice genuine transparency and to always inform John of the things he needed to know.

Over the next decade, it was her privilege and joy to serve him, she said. "John's greatest gift as headmaster was his caring spirit and love for people. He preferred spending time with students above all else." In his handling of many difficult situations that arose involving students and often their parents as well, Susan saw John's consistent prayer and wise counsel as the hallmarks of his headmastership. She noted that when students struggled or got into trouble—mostly in the upper school—their parents were unaware of how every meeting had been bathed in prayer as John and others tried to help the child. John often poured out his heart to a student and the parents of one who was going astray.

From Susan's perspective, John was the primary person in giving wise counsel. She never saw him give *un*wise counsel to a family, and he always tried to give the families hope that God can redeem a heart, a situation—or both. He invested in the students, Susan knew, and it broke her heart when students, and sometimes parents, refused to listen. In a few cases, however, the sense that an erring student felt in having disappointed the school's leadership, and more importantly the Lord, may have been worse than the consequence for the offense itself. In any case, Susan saw a number of students blessed when they listened to wise counsel: as the Scripture says, "*The way of a fool is right in his own eyes, But a wise man is he who listens to counsel*" (Proverbs 12:15); and, "*Through insolence comes nothing but strife, But wisdom is with those who receive counsel*" (Proverbs 13:10).

The godly wisdom Susan saw John consistently providing to students impacted her own family as well. As the Gaines's children—Austin

(ECS, 2009) and Collin (ECS, 2011), and their daughter, Lauren (ECS, 2013)—advanced through the ranks of the school, Susan was well aware of John Geiger constantly speaking into the lives of all three of them. Although her husband, John Gaines, had opportunities to accept a pastorate outside the Montgomery area, he and Susan made the difficult decision to remain where they were. Their decision was based on what their children were receiving at Eastwood. As Susan explained, John Geiger was a big part of that. So was Pastor Aaron Fleming, who devoted considerable time and energy to her boys, and Eastwood's youth director, Brian MacDonald, who discipled Austin.

School Matters and "Geiger's Gatherings"

Sometimes controversies arose over differences of opinion. When a number of students in the Class of 2009 wanted a particular teacher for one of their core courses in their upcoming senior year, they petitioned Mr. Geiger to change the assigned instructor. He met with the petitioning students and dealt with them in a dignified manner—but kept the original teacher.

In another, wearying case of dealing with controversy of one sort or another, John came home totally spent. He was met with little Nolin coming up to get his hug and saying to his dad, "Love your enemies and *pway* for those who persecute you." Dawn, who had not heard Nolin, was taken aback when John asked her, "Have you been talking to him?" "No," she replied. When it became clear Nolin was simply repeating his Bible verse for the week, John was relieved—but he also realized the Holy Spirit was at work in his heart regarding the trying situation at school.

Despite the need for counseling and problem-solving, the general tone of John's time with students and parents was positive. As Cynthia Jones expressed, "John loved being around parents and the students." He sought to meet with every parent in the school—Cynthia called them "Geiger's Gatherings"—although he sometimes had to rely on her timely texting of a parent's name who unexpectedly dropped by his office. He kept a Skittles dispenser on his desk to encourage students to come in, and he'd always have something to say to them. John was known to hold classes in his office, despite the accompanying drain on his Skittles supply.

In the Class of 2010's yearbook, an additional freebie was a color page entitled, "The Many Faces of Headmaster John Geiger," featuring John in no less than six different roles that he was known to fill in the life of ECS. The 2011 yearbook was dedicated to the memory of Virginia Foxworth Jacks, an ECS junior who died tragically in a vehicle accident in September 2010. As her classmates and friends wrote lovingly, "Virginia was no ordinary Christian. Her love for Christ overruled anything else that could have captured her heart."

Recollection: Faith (Beaulieu) Trent, Class of 2011

The graduating Class of 2011 contained 20 students, by far the largest up to that time (the next year's class had 26 graduates, the highest during John Geiger's tenure). Later, two of the 2011 graduates, Faith Trent and Jonathan Hilt, shared their recollections of Mr. Geiger. Faith, who went on to graduate with a nursing degree from Auburn University at Montgomery, and by 2020 was married, the mother of two, and a part-time labor-and-delivery nurse, recalled:

> Mr. Geiger loved telling and retelling the story of his proposal to Mrs. Geiger. He loved dwelling on beautiful things. I used to just watch Mr. and Mrs. Geiger together and relish how different they were; Mr. Geiger had a soft voice and paced speech and Mrs. Geiger is a very quick speaker, but never a thoughtless word escapes [her mouth]. With their shared thoughts, they spoke wisdom and truth that seemed to perfectly complement each other. They both shared an art of story telling and I still remember their stories today and apply the wisdom they so readily shared.[1]

Faith added a favorite memory of hers when, as a senior, she auditioned for the school play by singing a Simon and Garfunkel piece. Later

1 E-mail, Faith (Beaulieu) Trent to author, "Re: Memory of Mr. Geiger," Jan. 18, 2020.

that evening, her dad told her Mr. Geiger had found him "to tell him he thought I sang beautifully. It turns out our headmaster would hide out in the balcony for our play auditions! His good word towards me meant more than he knows."

Recollection: Jonathan Hilt, Class of 2011

Jonathan, who planned to return to Florida in 2011, recalled a conversation he had with Mr. Geiger in the Eastwood parking lot not long after graduation. Jonathan remembered it had begun as a short, "Hey man, how are you?" exchange that became an in-depth talk of half an hour. In a fatherly tone, Mr. Geiger said to him something like this:

> You know this already, Jonathan, but when you leave home, you learn things. You learn who you are. You learn who God is. And you learn where you fit into His story. But what you will soon know is that the world around you isn't a place to be afraid of; it's a place that will show you the most amazing things you have yet to see. Treasure it all and be thankful for what you've been given in this.[2]

Summertime

John thrived on opportunities for conversations like that one. It harkened of longtime ECS board chairman, and Eastwood elder, Allen McDaniel's recollection that over their years together he and John talked more *in the parking lot* than anywhere else, sometimes for an hour or longer. But such times came all too infrequently during the summer months for John's tastes. During June and July, John was at a loss, Cynthia and Susan agreed, because he didn't have people around him constantly to engage with. While the two ladies were trying to get ready for the upcoming school year—filing papers, building the calendar, updating the website, sending out transcripts—they'd *lock* the door to the school office. John would *unlock* the door. He wanted to see people. They wanted to get their work done. Somehow they managed.

---

2 E-mail, Jonathan Hilt to author, "Geiger Memory," Jan. 18, 2020.

At least John had an excellent diversion during a few of his summers. John had completed seminary in 1986 and was ordained as a minister (he also served as a ruling elder at Eastwood Presbyterian Church). His next older brother, Steve (second oldest of the five) and his wife, Diana, had three sons. John officiated their sons' weddings, in June 2007, June 2010, and May 2012. He also participated in the wedding of his nephew Matt, Bruce and Linda's oldest child. In each instance, John took his role as minister and uncle seriously and was honored to be asked to officiate. Thus, a family tradition continued—recalling that John's uncle, Rev. Oren Geiger, had officiated the wedding of his sister, LaRue, to John Hellenthal, in June 1945.

Eagle Scout Projects for ECS

Aside from those special events, there was student-led summer work that contributed to the school. Eastwood church sponsored Boy Scout Troop 924, most of whose members were ECS or Eastwood homeschool students. Troop 924 was very small but was skillfully led by Lee Sumner—an Eagle Scout himself—originally from Tifton, Georgia, and a U.S. Air Force Academy graduate and, later, an Eastwood elder. Untiringly, Lee kept his young men focused on working toward the coveted Eagle rank, which—rather amazingly—every boy who remained in the troop eventually achieved. At least five of them consulted with Mr. Geiger on Eagle project ideas to benefit the school. Troop 924's projects resulted in the flagpole (with lighting) situated on the school grounds (Michael Joki, ECS, 2009); renovated, painted student lockers in the upper school building (Nathan Marion, ECS, 2009); picnic tables in the church/school playground area (Samuel Sumner, Eastwood homeschool, 2009); benches in the playground area (Michael Knotts, ECS, 2011); and, several years later, an "Octaball" pit in the playground area (Jonathan Sumner, Eastwood homeschool, and a very young Eagle Scout not due to graduate until 2022).

2012 Yearbook Letter

For the Class of 2012's yearbook, John returned to some of his favorite themes in his letter to the school:

On March 24, 1944, 76 men escaped from a German prisoner-of-war camp called Stalag Luft III. This camp contained primarily American and British air force officers. These men had taken an oath that, if captured, they would endeavor to escape. The enemy went to extreme measures to prevent escape; so, how did these men do it? Tunnels. They dug three different tunnels named Tom, Dick, and Harry, approximately 30 feet below the surface and two feet tall by two feet wide. Harry, which was used in the escape, was around 300 feet long.

We admire a story of a group of imprisoned men who strive to gain their freedom. This theme of escape permeates history, literature, and popular culture. It is attractive to us. Edmond Dantès escapes from Chateau d'If in *The Count of Monte Cristo.* In the *Odyssey*, Ulysses, trapped in a cave by the Cyclops Polyphemus, escapes by skewering the giant's eye. Aeneas, with his father on his back, escapes from the burning city of Troy in the *Aeneid*. . . . We read these stories at Eastwood, and we are all attracted to the notion of escaping danger and gaining freedom. Why? I think it is because man, like those prisoners of war, is trapped, and he longs for freedom. But what is his prison? Spiritually, it is sin and the curse of death. Educationally, it is ignorance.

This is the theme of God's great story: man can be freed and escape from his sinful and fallen nature. Man will escape from the curse in the Garden of Eden. He will return to Paradise, but not on his own. He will need help. Thanks be to Christ Jesus who rescued man from his spiritual condition of death. In addition, man has the calling, as Milton says, "to repair the ruins." His ruined mind, through rigorous training and discipline, can be educated for the glory of God.[3]

Providing such mental training and discipline—and more, for God's glory—remained headmaster John Geiger's ambition.

3 [yearbook] *Eastwood Christian School 2011-2012*, 2.

12

John and ECS, 2012 to 2015

Bob Maruna: Upper School Principal

In the fall of 2011, John, with the school board's agreement, named Bob Maruna as the first ECS "upper school principal." Bob had served as church administrator since 1992 and the ECS administrator since 1996. He also taught physics in the upper school beginning with the 2005-2006 school year. During Bob's three years as upper school principal, he had closer contact with John than previously. He had long appreciated John's heart for people, whether a kindergartener or a high school senior or an international military officer or student. A number of officers from around the world attended courses at nearby Maxwell Air Force Base on a yearly basis, and on several occasions the Geigers hosted "internationals" for lengthy periods (including three Polish students in the ECS Class of 2017). Bob observed, perhaps even more than previously, that John was "always dressing up," which in the opinion of the Marunas' two sons, A.J. (Class of 2011) and Jack (Class of 2014), helped to make him "the perfect headmaster." Others seemed to share that view, and one ECS teacher referred to John as "a grown-up Nolin" in that sense (Nolin being John and Dawn's younger son).

More importantly, in a conversation at a favorite diner in Cincinnati the month after John's death, Bob shared that John "always carried with him a 'big world' perspective" especially relative to the need for the gospel. Bob "always felt like John was a trusted confidant" and one of the few with whom he could share whatever was on his heart and not feel judged. He pondered how many other men might have been able to say the same thing about John.

Recollection: Victoria (Foster) Whatley, Class of 2013

The upper school principal was not the only one to recall an incident or practice in which John's care for them was evident. An ECS graduate in the Class of 2013—one of several 13-year graduates that year (going from K through 12th grade at Eastwood)—Victoria Whatley treasured a particular memory that John often reminded her of. When she was about five years old, Victoria's dad was renovating the ECS school office, and he brought his daughter with him to work. Mr. Geiger was there and he engaged young Victoria in conversation at the office. It was a mundane incident, but it also was one that John used a number of times in later years—most likely with intent—to help break the ice for Victoria, at school or at church, whenever he had the opportunity of introducing her to someone new. In 2020, Victoria continued working for the State of Alabama (since 2013); she also was married and the mother of a young daughter.

Allen McDaniel: ECS Board Chairman

Allen McDaniel, who served far more than his share of the academic years through the spring of 2014 as ECS board chairman, agreed with Bob Maruna's perspective, acknowledging John's "big, Christian worldview." Allen noted that very often, if John could get an audience with a parent who was willing to listen to his "pitch" on classical Christian education and how ECS implemented that model, they'd be "sold" on the concept and seek enrollment for their child. He was a great "vision-caster."

Allen also recalled that John liked to cook. Once, Allen picked up some seafood at Costco for John during the store's annual Christmas sale. That Christmas, John brought fish chowder that he had prepared to the McDaniel home—and he did so regularly thereafter at Christmastime. In 2019—as John was sending out some of his final, gracious communications via text, only two weeks before his death—Nolin brought the chowder.

Recollection: Julie McDaniel, Class of 2015

Allen and Linda McDaniel's youngest of five children, Julie, graduated with the Class of 2015—completing a five-for-five record for her and her siblings as ECS graduates. One of Julie's recollections of Mr. Geiger was that he held classes in several different places besides the regular classroom, including the youth room, session room, and his own office. Students enjoyed the informality which also facilitated more open discussion. Sometimes he'd bring his guitar and play a song or two. For Monday morning assemblies, John had a knack for taking a mundane experience or observation (often from nature) from the week prior and using it to illustrate some aspect of God's kindness or mercy. As was the family tradition, Julie continued on to Auburn University and pharmacy school.

Julie remembered that her class trip to Europe was the largest one so far (17 seniors) and that Mr. Geiger conducted many of the tour-guide talks at the various sites they visited. He was always the last one of the group to board the train or vehicle taking them to wherever. She concluded that was so that no student, unfamiliar with whichever European city they were in, might panic in the case of failing to board in time: it was a small but very real act of modern-day chivalry.

2013 Senior Trip: "Carry on, I'll find you guys."

Julie's observation had precedent. On the 2013 class trip to Europe, one of the seniors realized she had forgotten her bag of mementos at a double-decker carousel (near Notre Dame Cathedral) just as the doors were about to close on the Paris subway. In a flash—and as longtime Latin and science teacher David Miller recalled vividly—John jumped off the subway and called out, "Carry on, I'll find you guys." The doors closed immediately. David's clear recollection was that, with John's departure from the group, *he* was now in charge (Dawn also knew Paris well but she missed that trip). It was only his second trip to Europe and John had handled all the details of the itinerary, including contingency plans in case a particular subway became unavailable, perhaps due to some not-infrequent labor strike. Suddenly, David had to decipher the Paris Metro (with some three hundred lines) in order to navigate the group first to the Arc de Triomphe, followed by a walk to the renowned museum, the Musée du Louvre.

Finding their way to the arch, David reasoned the best place to wait for John, to ensure they didn't miss him, was at the top (they would miss each other if one was going *up on one side* of the arch while the other came *down on the other side*). Meanwhile, John had retrieved the mementos and made his way to the arch, but aware of the same potential (as David realized) to miss the group, he decided to wait for them at the bottom. David outwaited John. With no sign of John, and some of the seniors—all girls on this trip—getting weepy with concern for Mr. Geiger, David decided to strike out for the Louvre. Arriving there, he was leading them through a section with various sculptures and explaining about them, while in the back of his mind wondering if he needed to call the Paris police or Dawn regarding John's whereabouts. Suddenly, several students gasped and immediately David felt a pat on his shoulder from behind. It was John; as David related, somehow in the mass of humanity at the Louvre, he found us! Another teacher, upon hearing the story, likened it to a kind of superhero episode. En effet (indeed).

Recollection: Amelia Rhodes, Class of 2015

Another 2015 graduate, Amelia Rhodes, treasured a memory of Mr. Geiger from her senior class trip. In Paris, after the ECS group had completed an exhausting trek to the top of the Eiffel Tower (669 steps to the top), the next stop was the Arc de Triomphe, commissioned by Napoleon I and one of the best-known monuments of Western Civilization (at times the triumphant one has been feared and despised, as in 1940 when Hitler reveled there following his stunning victory over the French army). Unlike two years earlier, in 2015 the ECS group managed to stay together! The Eastwood group of about two dozen had planned to ascend to the top of this famous structure as well—but it required trudging an additional 284 steps. Amelia was tired and felt quite willing to enjoy this site from the ground. While the rest of the group ascended, John stayed behind with her. They walked a few yards to a sidewalk café, and, away from the bustle of the arch, the two of them shared a Coca-Cola from a bottle with straws together, and just talked.

After ECS, Amelia attended the University of Mississippi ("Ole Miss"), and by the spring of 2020 she had completed a bachelor's degree in Elementary Education and master's degree in Curriculum and Instruction. Reflecting that year on the time she had enjoyed one-on-one with John Geiger in Paris, five years earlier, made for a sweet memory.

2015 Yearbook Letter, and Victor Davis Hanson's *Carnage and Culture*

Whether or not he realized how much the one-on-one time with his seniors meant to them, John's words to the school's families in his end-of-year (yearbook) letter recalled the recent trip to Europe; through Rome, Paris, Normandy, London, and Cambridge. He wrote:

> It is a capstone for their education. They had studied ideas and read books full of ideas; now, they were able to see and touch the consequences of those very ideas that helped to shape Western Civilization. An Eastwood education helped them appreciate and understand what they saw. It helped them to think biblically about the ideas they confronted in art and architecture.[1]

The ECS senior trips to Europe also went hand-in-hand with something important that noted historian Victor Davis Hanson has highlighted. Beginning with the Greek city states some two thousand five hundred years ago, certain cultural traits spread to western and northern Europe and, through colonization, to other parts of the world, and came to characterize in part what we call Western civilization.

1 [yearbook] *Eastwood Christian School, 2015*, 2.

The ownership of small, independent farms facilitated many ordinary Greek men—especially heads of household—subjecting themselves voluntarily to military discipline in elements usually organized as heavy infantry and that placed a high value on competence, cohesion, audit, and accountability. Hanson writes, "Western armies often fight with and for a sense of legal freedom. They are frequently products of civic militarism or constitutional governments and thus are overseen by those outside religion and the military itself. The rare word 'citizen' exists in the *European* vocabularies."[2]

What does this have to do with Eastwood students, you may ask? A number of traditional American cultural traits, still held in high regard in many homes, churches, entities, and communities across the land, are quite inseparable from the Western way of war that Hanson describes. The competence—or *professionalism*, in today's parlance—of Western armies has been foundational to the civic life of Western societies. Competence is a cultural *given* in the West—it is assumed, or it was until recently. Eastwood students are taught to aspire to high *competence* (or excellence) in their studies, arts, athletics, and more, doing all things to the glory of God. In the America of 2020, the unambiguous affirmation of the enduring value of a number of Western ideals—taught in the Scriptures as well—deserves to be stated explicitly.

In addition to high *competence*, the habits of *audit*, *accountability*, and the *cohesion* of Western armies, witnessed in countless engagements including at Rorke's Drift in January 1879—in which no more than one hundred British riflemen remained intact, supported one another and fought as one, and so held off *four thousand* Zulu warriors—are reflected in myriad contexts in Western civic life to this day, extending even to a

---

2 Victor Davis Hanson, *Carnage and Culture: Landmark Battles in the Rise of Western Power* (Doubleday: New York and London, 2001), preface, 21 (emphasis added). The origin of the important term "citizen" is suggested by the fifth-century Greek historian, Thucydides, who wrote of some of those who relocated from other parts of Greece to Athens and who "became citizens"; see Rex Warner, trans., *Thucydides: History of the Peloponnesian War* (Penguin Books: London and New York, 1972 [1954]), 36. The author of the New Testament's Book of Hebrews, in chapter 8, verse 11, also used the word 'citizen' (from the Greek translation of the Old Testament's Book of Jeremiah).

classical Christian school in Montgomery, Alabama. (Some may be surprised to learn that a number of *assumed* traits in the West, including audit and accountability, generally are not regarded in the non-West, where ethnic and kinship loyalties are more highly valued.)[3] When an ECS student is held accountable, for instance, it is in many ways a legacy of Western armies and the civilization those armies buttressed.[4]

3 In addition, the U.S. military's advisory experience since 2001 in places such as Afghanistan and Iraq have provided painful lessons of the fact that in the non-West, assumed Western values often are superseded by other traits.

4 Hanson, *Carnage and Culture*, chapter 8. The Zulu warriors—like many non-Western fighters over the last two millennia—were valiant warriors *individually*, but they lacked the ability to fight as a cohesive, united-in-action, force. Had they done so, they must have annihilated the small British force.

Fox Theatre, Visalia, California, ca. 1940s, and Robert and Dorothy Geiger's anniversary, 2002.

The Geiger "Band of Brothers" at Christmastime, ca. 1966.

Geiger Family with older boys, ca 1975.

First day of travel from Anchorage, Steve/John's trip back to Visalia, "Alaska John" in front of Matanuska Glacier, Mar. 31, 1979.

John skiing at Heavenly Valley (Lake Tahoe, California), winter of 1979-1980.

"Quarter Hour of Power" team: Richard Minkler, Gene Antonio, John Geiger, ca. 1980.

Dating. ca. 1987.

John with Soren and Mary Agnes in Moscow (one of the "Seven Sisters" in the background), ca. 1995.

John, Soren and Mary Agnes on a Russian tank during a "patriotic" celebration in Moscow, ca. 1995.

Students turning John into a human sundae, ca. 1998.

John officiating the wedding of his nephew (Erik) and his bride (Lindsay), Woodlake, California, May 26, 2012.

Dawn and John in Rome atop the Castel Sant'Angelo with St Peter's Basilica in the background, Mar. 2015.

Dawn and John sitting on the plexiglass panels of the Eiffel Tower high above the streets of Paris, Mar. 2015. (Not John's favorite Senior Trip activity.)

John singing with kindergarteners, ca. 2016.

"Zeus" addressing the competing teams for Olympic Field Day, ca. 2016.

Roman soldier "Gluteus Maximus" (Joel Bius) who guarded the Apostle Paul (John Geiger) during Vacation Bible School, Jun. 2017.

The Band of Brothers in front of German artillery gun emplacement on Pointe du Hoc, Sept. 2018. From left: Steve, Paul, Bruce, John and Greg.

Last Breath Tour tee-shirts with Mike and Cheryl Kometer and their son Mikey, 2018.

At the home of David and Kathryn Lohnes in Le Déluge, France, with Wiktor Poznachowski and Tim and Szon Tomkiewicz, 2018.

John with Nolin in front of the Eiger mountain while visiting Pastor Stephen Spanjer, Mürren, Switzerland, Oct. 2018.

Steve and Michelle Wilson visit from Kansas City, Kansas, 2019. (John and Steve worked together in the Fathering Ministry in Ukraine.)

John and Dawn enjoy grandparenting as they ride in the golf cart with Evelyn Walker (daughter of Mary Agnes and Eric) and Leo Geiger (son of Soren and Virginia), 2019.

John resting his head on his cane as he listens to a conversation, ca. 2019.

13

John and ECS, 2015 to 2017

David Givens: Upper School Principal

In the fall of 2016, John and the school board elevated longtime Latin teacher David Givens to ECS upper school principal. Previously, Bob Maruna had served his last three years at Eastwood in that role (2011-2014); then, for the next two years John Geiger managed double-duty as headmaster *and* upper school principal.

In 2002, David had returned to his hometown of Montgomery following his graduation from Hillsdale College in Michigan. In the fall of that year, he began as a part-time Latin teacher in the upper school at ECS and soon became convinced that God wanted him to pursue teaching for his career. Sometime during the spring of 2003, an in-depth conversation he had with John strengthened David's conviction about God's call as a teacher. With the next school year, David became one of the few full-time ECS teachers and began taking on additional duties, including coaching the boys' basketball team.

From the fall of 2003 until John Geiger's retirement in 2018, David and John spent a lot of time together, especially in the context of the upper school where John also taught. Both men's lives were enmeshed with the school, especially as their wives also taught and their children were students there (one of David's kids once quipped, "School *is* home").

David had plenty of opportunities to observe and interact with John in activities ranging from teacher training sessions, staff meetings, and school assemblies (including John's devotionals) to special events (including Medieval Games and school plays) to conversations during the course of a normal school day. For a time, David's parents lived on "the hill," where the Geigers and Nolins (Dawn's parents) lived, and so David saw John and his family in an ordinary household setting, too. In February 2019, David shared some well-seasoned thoughts of his headmaster, fellow teacher, and friend: "John had a way of looking at everything through spiritual eyes and in a way that few people do." Long before his ALS diagnosis, John looked for ways to redeem each conversation, David noted, and, "He had that ability to see things with a redeemed mind . . . [and knowing that] it's about God working through the word of Christ in everything that we do now. . . . He had a mind for the redemption of the mundane."

One such case occurred in the fall of 2017 when David and John decided to go for an "old-school shave" at the Chop Shop, located downtown on Dexter Avenue. Agreeing to meet at the shop on a Saturday morning, David picked up coffee for the two of them. The barber, a master at his craft which involved an ample amount of shaving cream and a finely honed razor, took his time with each man. They had the shop to themselves, providing the opportunity for good conversation. David's kids were with him, and, impressed with the almost sacred nature of these moments for their dad and his older friend, sat and watched in silence. Near the end of the time, John commented on how there is something good in seeing someone do what they do well. David recalled John saying, "It's a testament to who God is and the gifts He's given us . . . there's something good about functioning in your gift." David viewed his words as "a recognition of the truth in that moment" and making it known in a way that pointed toward God's grace in an everyday event.

Recollection: Margaret Rhodes, Class of 2017

The mundane included visits to ECS classrooms. Margaret Rhodes, a 13-year student at ECS, had known Mr. Geiger as long as she could remember. As a lower school student, Margaret recalled he was the favorite one to come into a classroom. He knew the kids' names and often brought his guitar as well as a story or two. When she moved into the upper school, Margaret saw him almost every day and got to know him better. As others have expressed, Margaret had never met a teacher like Mr. Geiger, and "he always knew the right thing to say." She and John shared a love for hunting and they talked about that. He was an "old-school hunter" who had not used a scope in his younger days when he hunted out West.

The eight students who went on the senior class trip in the spring of 2017 were all girls. Margaret said it was the best trip of her life, and she especially enjoyed the visit with David and Kathryn Lohnes in France. The long-lasting and deep friendship between the Geigers and Lohneses made for some wonderful stories while at the Lohneses' home. Following graduation from Eastwood, Margaret continued a family tradition by attending Huntingdon College in Montgomery, where, as of 2020 she was majoring in Sports Management with a minor in Business.

Recollection: Erin Powe, Class of 2017

Another senior on the class trip was Erin Powe. She remembered John and Dawn typically led the pack at the various sites they visited, which was impressive to her considering how much walking the group did. At one picnic site by a sheep pasture—where the group enjoyed the view of Mont Saint-Michel—Pastor David Lohnes led the students in a French blessing before the meal. There was a "guys' part" and a "girls' part," Erin said; given the makeup of the group the guys' part had to be sung vigorously by only three—David, John, and upper school teacher David Miller (on his fourth trip to Europe since 2012 and now much more confident on the Paris Metro than on 2013's unforgettable trip).

As graduation approached, all the seniors gave their speeches at one of several venues in a relatively small gathering, but Erin was one of the three who was to present her speech on graduation night—for a second time—before a full crowd in the Eastwood sanctuary. With her first presentation, she had been way too fast, she remembered, and Mr. Geiger worked with her patiently to help her slow down. Her speech's theme was from C. S. Lewis's *The Horse and His Boy*. Erin commented on John's well-known affection for his "white board," which he used in this case to help her plan her speech. He also liked to use the board to remind students to "stay tethered" to the truth, by drawing a kite and a string. Whenever he could possibly use the white board, Erin noted, he'd use it.

Thinking back to her earlier years at ECS, Erin recalled her own emotional struggles. In that difficult period John had made her feel loved, on one occasion by noticing Erin's Facebook post of her new BB-gun and using that to begin a conversation with her which then turned to deeper concerns. As of 2020, Erin attended Auburn University and was majoring in English Literature.

Denise Brassell: Retirement and Remembrance

As the Class of 2017 prepared to graduate, the school's longest-serving and beloved upper school teacher—Denise Brassell—departed also, to a well-earned retirement. From the fall of 1996—ECS's opening—through the spring of 2017, Denise taught mathematics and sciences in the upper school. She also served as the upper school director for 8 years. Three years after retiring, when contacted about John's biography, she shared these thoughts:

> John was like the older brother to me that I never had but always wished for. While we did not always see eye-to-eye on things, I like to think that as iron sharpens iron, John and I did that for each other personally and professionally during the nearly [20] years we worked together.
>
> Many may not know that while John focused much of his teaching efforts on the humanities, he equally loved and appreciated math and the sciences. He would oftentimes visit my classroom to participate in science experiments or to view the beautiful process of solving an algebra or geometry problem.

> John even let me "tag team" teach American Literature with him for several years. During that time I learned a great deal about writing and learning to love literature even though my left-brained self was more geared to mathematics and science. John was also adept at computer skills and would often show me shortcuts to help with programs about which I was unfamiliar. . . . He pushed me to be better just as he did his students.[1]

Denise closed her thoughtful recollection, noting that she and John had "worked at doing what we both loved—teaching children from a godly perspective. From Medieval Day to video parodies of our students to teaching teachers to be the best they could be, I will always have fond memories of the work John and I co-labored in at Eastwood." Her words were illuminating and a fitting reminder of the scripture to which she alluded, "*Iron sharpens iron, so one man sharpens another*" (Proverbs 27:17).

1 E-mail, Denise Brassell to author, "Re: Chapter—John's bio," May 8, 2020.

14

Prelude to Passing the Torch

"Paul the Apostle" and "Gluteus Maximus"

For years John engaged in song, drama, and even silliness at times in order to gain an audience with those to whom he sought to communicate truth, beauty, and love. In perhaps the most poignant example, for Eastwood Presbyterian Church's Vacation Bible School (VBS) program in 2017 he took on the role of the Apostle Paul. The VBS theme that summer was from the Book of Acts, focusing on Paul and the early Church and their dealings with the Roman Empire. The plan for the week included Paul (played by John G.) as a prisoner for the gospel, "chained" to a Roman soldier—played by fellow church member and U.S. Air Force officer, Lieutenant Colonel Joel Bius. Joel had wanted to participate in VBS and finally had the chance to do so, but he and John hardly knew each other prior to that week. Joel's older sons, Jake and Brooks, who were helping out, and John's younger son, Nolin, figured Joel needed a good Latin name. They came up with "Gluteus Maximus," which probably went over the heads of the younger children but was greatly enjoyed by the older generation! Paul, the prisoner, had an authentic-looking "cell" (a converted Sunday School room), where his Roman guard, Maximus, watched over him. They were chained together, as in Roman times (perhaps alluded to in Acts 28:16, *"And when we entered Rome, Paul was allowed to stay by himself, with the soldier who was guarding him"*).

At the start of the week, Gluteus Maximus was a mean, rough soldier who treated his prisoner poorly and had little but contempt for the gospel. He carried a sword, wore a helmet, and was unshaven. Joel's wife, Leigh, added eye shadow to his face to make Maximus look even scarier to the children—fifth graders and younger. He yelled at the kids trying to sneak food to the prisoner, as Paul (John) tried to calm them by explaining that he was a prisoner for the gospel of Christ and that everything was alright. Probably he alluded to some of Paul's words such as in his last epistle before being martyred: *"I suffer hardship even to imprisonment as a criminal; but the word of God is not imprisoned" (2 Timothy 2:9).* As the week progressed, Maximus softened to the gospel message he had heard over and over as Paul spoke to each group of children who visited him in prison. The soldier began saying to Paul, as the children watched: "Hey, I've heard you say this stuff over and over, tell me more about it."

By Thursday, the children were getting excited and wondering whether the Roman soldier was going to become a Christian. There was a scandal of sorts in the community in that a Christian young woman had recently had a baby, and the rumor was that the father was none other than the as-yet-unconverted Maximus. In real life, Joel and Leigh's young son, John Henry, was only three months' old, so their "scandal" meshed perfectly into the VBS storyline as the baby appeared in his mother's arms—and bore a striking resemblance to Maximus!

John's Phone Call

Also on Thursday, John had to leave early from VBS. He was to receive a phone call from his doctor about a medical condition. Joel adjusted the storyline for the children, who again were to visit the prison cell and of course would wonder where Paul was. Maximus told them the prisoner had been summoned to appear before a Roman court that day. He also used his opportunity with the children—without the apostle beside him—to ask them: "You know all this stuff Paul has been saying, do you really believe that?"

On Friday—with no one at VBS aware of the true nature of the phone call the day prior—John showed up and rolled right back into his role as the apostle. Joel recalled seeing no difference in his demeanor from the day before. The last day's theme was to be one of great joy, as Maximus had prayed long and hard the night before. He had realized his sinfulness and that he was justly deserving of divine wrath and judgment. Maximus had believed upon Jesus Christ, turned from his life of sin and received the pardon for all his sins provided in Jesus alone—the Suffering Servant whom Paul had preached faithfully in his presence throughout the week. To highlight his new nature in Christ, Maximus appeared on Friday clean-shaven and without his helmet and sword. In January 2020, shortly after John's homegoing, Joel recalled that, with genuine joy, John—as the Apostle Paul—had told the children that Friday morning that he had great news for them. His friend, the Roman soldier, Gluteus Maximus, had become a Christian!

Joel continued, noting that in the VBS script John had played a man who was likely facing a *death sentence*. It was shortly after VBS ended when Joel, and the rest of the Eastwood church and school community, became aware that John had received what might be termed "a real death sentence" with the diagnosis of ALS—for which there was no cure. That was the Thursday phone call. John had said nothing about it.

Joel was impressed not only with John's ability to finish out the VBS program, but also with "how natural it was for him to share the joy of salvation" in Christ with the children as he explained to them what had happened to his Roman guard. Joel also was impressed with Nolin and with his and John's relationship as he observed their mutual affection. On several breaks that week, Nolin came running into his dad's jail cell and jumped into his lap. There was a genuine relationship and affection between them. Especially in today's culture, many dads and their sons—even young teenagers—could learn much from their example.

Joel and Leigh Bius: Seeing Seeds Planted, Bearing Fruit

In 2020, Joel recollected on how his time with John had impacted him in another sense. Joel viewed himself as a man probably at the halfway point of his life. He wanted to be focused rightly on those priorities that mattered most and to finish well the race set before him. John's obvious affection for Nolin and the young children were impressive to him, affections borne out all the more in his manner of speech with them. Joel noted that he and John had been given a script for the week—but they never used it. Everything John said to the children who visited his jail cell came from the heart.

But there was another aspect to the one-week intensive relationship of John Geiger and Joel Bius. Neither man could have known it at the time, but the Spirit of the Sovereign God was quietly at work, using John to plant a seed in Joel's mind that was to bear fruit shortly after John's death three years later. It was the prelude to a passing of the torch. As they spent time together that week over the lengthy breaks between the groups of children who visited Paul in prison, John and Joel talked about many things—among them the classical Christian education model, and the school at Eastwood. It was completely natural for John to share glimpses of his vision for the education model that was being worked out in the lives of the young men and women at ECS, including some of the accompanying joys and challenges. By their sharing such extended time together, Joel gained insight into a model that previously was unknown to him, and he began to envision the things God might accomplish through such a program within the bounds of his local church and community.

That seed was nurtured, and in early 2020, as Joel prepared to retire from the U.S. Air Force, both he and Leigh became convinced that God wanted him to apply for the ECS headmaster position from which John had retired in 2018. An Eastwood men's breakfast at the start of 2020 was partly responsible for Joel's growing conviction. He was encouraged by the speaker, Eastwood elder and ECS school board chairman Jeff Dunn, to be willing to trust God with the kind of *unknown* that Joel had begun to consider. In a parallel to Joel's situation, several years earlier Colonel Dunn had retired from the Air Force to assume significant responsibilities in an arena entirely new to him—of all things, as the commissioner over the State of Alabama's prison system. Joel applied for the ECS job, and in March 2020 Dr. Joel R. Bius was announced as the new headmaster. Unknown to John and Joel, that transition had begun three years earlier while "chained" together for a week of Vacation Bible School.

There was yet another poignant aspect to the Bius family's transition that no man could have foreseen. Years earlier, when Joel's wife, Leigh—well prior to their relationship—had worked at Faulkner University in Montgomery, she had been involved with the school's "great books" program. Guest speakers visited Faulkner and talked with the students about their books and their worldviews. On several occasions, she noticed a small group of noticeably younger students in the back of the auditorium, wearing uniforms and well-behaved, sitting together and soaking in the talks. She wondered who they were. She learned they were ECS upper school students, accompanied by their headmaster, John Geiger. Leigh was so impressed that she told herself, basically, "If I ever get married and have children, I'd want them to go to a school like Eastwood." In the fall of 2020, the Bius's second youngest, Mary Jewel, began kindergarten at ECS. Plans were for her younger brother, John Henry—of VBS 2017 fame—to follow her the next year.

15

Last Year at ECS, and "Reflections" Ministry

Diagnosis of ALS

In the summer of 2017, John and Dawn learned, after extensive medical testing, that John was suffering from Amyotrophic Lateral Sclerosis, or ALS. Also known as Lou Gehrig's disease—Gehrig, of New York Yankees' fame, abruptly retired from baseball in 1939 when he was diagnosed, bringing worldwide attention to the disease; he died in 1941 at thirty-seven—ALS is a neurodegenerative disease that typically affects upper and lower motor neurons and causes degeneration of the brain and spinal cord. While a small percentage of ALS cases are passed genetically from one generation to the next, the vast majority of cases appear "spontaneously and mysteriously . . . on previously healthy adults," according to an ALS state chapter association. A cure "still remains elusive."[1] Beginning with their family, church session, and Eastwood Christian School, the Geigers broke the news to each group with grace and gentleness, while continuing to express

1 ALS Wisconsin Chapter Association, "What is ALS?," *www.alsawi.org*, accessed Jun. 8, 2020.

their trust in the Lord Jesus Christ and in His compassion, wisdom, and sufficiency for their every need.

Last Year at ECS

If his health permitted it, John wanted to finish up one final year as headmaster and as a teacher at ECS. He did so, leading and participating in—as he had done for a decade and a half—all of the traditional events that the school's students and families, and faculty and staff, had enjoyed. For certain events, the headmaster was known to appear in the persona of Zeus or Quasimodo, which technique John had learned gave him an attentive audience for the message he sought to convey to his students. In one particular example of God's kindness both to John and to Eastwood's upper school students, a last-minute teaching vacancy provided John the opportunity to teach the required Bible course to *every* class of upper school students in what was to be his last year at the school. A gifted teacher, John poured himself into his students, many of whom probably were motivated to hear what he had to say, knowing his words were the conclusions and convictions of a man who loved them and God's Word and whose earthly course was winding down. In the early fall of 2018, looking back, John said, "I wanted to give my last year to the kids."

Recollection: Leila Vaughn, Class of 2018

One of several 13-year ECS students, Leila Vaughn had several favorite memories of her headmaster. One of them originated with John's unique way of bringing music and song into his classes (sometimes his own songs) in order to promote discussion of the songwriter's views. Leila especially liked a song by Randy Stonehill called "Shut De Do," which John taught to her class. When the students expressed interest in seeing him in concert, John agreed. They thought he was kidding them. Instead, John managed to arrange a trip to a small church near Pelham, Alabama, where his students heard Randy sing. Leila also appreciated Mr. Geiger's willingness to grapple with off-topic questions, and his honesty whenever he lacked an adequate response in the moment.

When it came to her senior speech, Leila's greatest challenge wasn't so much the fear of public speaking, but of talking "really fast," she confessed.

John worked with her to slow down, in large part by over-dramatizing with his own s-l-o-w speech and motions as he provided her with feedback and suggestions. As of 2020, Leila was midway through a bachelor's degree in Art at Covenant College, situated on beautiful Lookout Mountain, Georgia.

Recollection: John "Nolin" Geiger, Class of 2018

From Nolin's perspective, even though his dad had been diagnosed with ALS, things were "pretty normal" that school year. John still was walking and driving on his own. On the senior trip, he went to all the sites with the seniors but rather than walking the hundreds of steps for the full view at some of them—for example, at the Arc de Triomphe—he found a bench or a café to sit and rest. At the church that David Lohnes pastored, whose congregation the Geigers and ECS enjoyed close relations with, John shared his Reflections of a Dying Christian. David translated into French for his congregation. In order to maximize his remaining time with his dad, after graduation from ECS Nolin remained at home and as of 2020 was taking courses at Faulkner University in Montgomery.

Perhaps it was an earlier year when Nolin and one or both of his older siblings decided it was time for an intervention of sorts regarding their dad's lack of fashion sense. John, like many men, didn't like to shop and when forced to do it often found himself buying several of the same thing, only different colors. As John related, his kids had complained, "Dad, get some new shorts, you're embarrassing us." John dutifully made his way to a clothing store and found some shorts he liked well enough to buy. He happened to look down at what he was wearing and—you guessed it—they were the same shorts he was about to buy, "the exact same brand and model," he recalled. He thought to himself, "Boy, am I in a rut," and the kids enjoyed a good laugh when he sent them a picture of the shorts and shared the incident with them. John commented:

> As a father, you know how your children enjoy some of *your* idiosyncrasies. They make fun of 'em, it's part of the family tradition. . . . One of the wretched aspects of death is that it steals from the family the little joys that our children have. . . . Death

is an enemy that steals, and we never should call it anything but what it is. It will be a vanquished foe, but it's a foe.[2]

Closing his thoughts on this little window into family life—not only his own family, but generally—John said of the children, simply: "They love that, they love that."

David Miller's London Recollection

On the trip to Europe in the spring of 2018—John's last senior trip—David Miller had the opportunity to observe John in an unusual setting. It was the end of a grueling trip with a large group of seniors (15). They had made it to London and were preparing to fly home. David needed some down-time and had found refuge for the evening—so he thought—in the hotel bar. It was not to be. Instead of some quiet relaxation over a cold drink, David found a Welshman in the nearly deserted bar desperate to tell someone how well his business was doing that week. David became his audience. The already fatigued Eastwood chaperone heard far more than he ever wanted to know about the man's business—which was delivering "luxury port-a-potties . . . to movie sets"—and how well things were going. Finally, unable to stand it any longer, David excused himself in the most civil manner he could muster in the moment and retreated to the corner with his drink. A little later, in walked John Geiger. John noticed David smoldering in the corner and could tell he needed to be left alone. To David's amazement, it wasn't more than one minute or so before John was talking to the Welshman—the "king of port-a-potties"—about the gospel. Soon after that, the man confessed to John his need for a change in his life; the only one he had ever trusted in to get the job done had been himself. When John shared with him that he was dying from ALS, the man teared up, hugged John, and they exchanged e-mails. As David well said, it was convicting, amazing, and powerful to be around John Geiger.

2 Interview, John E. Geiger with author, Montgomery, Ala., Sep. 8, 2018.

A Knight to Celebrate

Undoubtedly the high point of John's last year with Eastwood school was a secretly-planned (he claimed no knowledge of it), music-, drama-, and testimony-filled event held one night in early April 2018 that celebrated John's life and ministry. He had been told to set aside that evening because the students were going to sing some songs. At that, John rolled his eyes—he was unexcited about the type of music he anticipated hearing—but he agreed. On the night of the event, some six to seven hundred present-day and former students, families, and church members packed out the Eastwood church sanctuary and were encouraged by being together with John and his family, to honor him and most of all to be reminded of the promises of the gospel. The event was called, appropriately, "A Knight to Celebrate."

"Reflections of a Dying Christian"

Also during the 2017-2018 academic year, the Lord gave John the opportunity to speak to several dozen groups—mainly churches and private school gatherings but also civic groups—mostly in the Montgomery area but also in other parts of Alabama and as far away as Tennessee. His typical address, "Reflections of a Dying Christian," began with a small men's study led by a like-minded physician friend in town, Dr. Matt Phillips, who invited John to share with them. Soon after, he spoke with his Eastwood students on the same theme. The word was getting out about John's talk. He and Dawn quickly found themselves with invitations to local churches on an almost weekly basis. Some were churches they had not even heard of (Montgomery has a lot of churches!). John found the experience to be a wonderful outreach opportunity.

As John recounted in late 2018, his "Reflections" ministry was ironic in that when he moved from southern California and settled in Alabama almost half his lifespan (three decades) earlier, he had not understood Southern men at all. His learning curve with them had been a long one, and even in 2018 he wasn't certain he understood them all that well. But, regardless, John found that every place he went to speak, the men accepted him, as different from them as he might be, as one who loved them. Over roughly a seven-month period, John spoke to some thirty to forty, mostly church, groups, usually on Sundays (mornings, evenings) or Wednesday nights.

The gatherings ranged, literally, from eight hundred persons to just eight, John said, and many who came were the elderly and the sick. Many seemed to wonder, John noticed, "What good am I? What is life's purpose now?" John appreciated that he was seeing a portion of many churches' flocks that often remained hidden. Ministering to them and offering himself as an example of one who—although dying—was still able and willing to reach out to others with the message of the resurrected Savior, was, he said in his now-gravelly but still-sonorous voice, "not glamorous, but very rewarding." He added, "What is your role in the kingdom? Where are you stationed to be faithful? No retreat!"

John began referring to his speaking engagements as his "Last Breath Tour." He had a faithful following of friends who often showed up to pray for and support him when he was speaking, regardless of the venue. He began lovingly calling them his "groupies," and he had "Dylan-esque" tee-shirts made for them to show his appreciation. His friend Mike Kometer, a retired U.S. Air Force colonel, and his wife Cheryl and son Mikey, were among his most loyal groupies. John often quipped that Mike could step in and do the talk for him if he needed him to. As Dawn lovingly observed, "Only John could position himself into the role of a rock star rather than a victim of a fatal and debilitating disease."

His unassuming manner and approach, according to one pastor and friend, was quite "disarming." Many attendees probably came to the event with a somewhat curious if not a wait-and-see attitude. John spoke of his life and of God's gracious work in his heart as a young man before moving on to his adult years, sharing glimpses of himself as a husband, father, missionary, and teacher. John admired many of the timeless military virtues such as devotion to duty, honor, self-sacrifice, and courage. He had come to identify closely with a British Army officer during World War Two, Brigadier Claude Nicholson who, in May 1940, on Churchill's order, resisted the Germans at Calais as long as possible without knowing fully *why*. Nicholson became a prisoner of war and died in German captivity in 1943. During the night of May 25/26, 1940, Churchill had sent a message to him that stated:

> Every hour you continue to exist is of the greatest help to the [British Expeditionary Force]. Government has therefore decided you must continue to fight. Have greatest possible admiration for your splendid stand. Evacuation will not (repeat not) take place. . . .[3]

Nicholson's skill, valor, and leadership in holding out for a full day after Calais had fallen to the Germans enabled the Allies to evacuate many more men from Dunkirk than if he had surrendered his force once it was clear that his situation was hopeless. Like Brigadier Nicholson at Calais in 1940, John Geiger was committed to holding out—for a purpose greater than himself—to the end. Many listeners seemed receptive to his message.

As John made clear, each person was dying, but what made him different was that he had a more definitive timetable given to him than others. Former ECS board member (including chairman for a time) and Eastwood church elder, Glenn Draper, recalled an address in May 2018. Speaking at Mountain Brook Community Church, in Birmingham, Alabama, John said "we were all like an airplane and that he himself didn't have much fuel left, and the issue with all of us was we didn't know how much fuel we each had left, and the point he made was [to] live every day for Christ because one day your fuel will run out."[4] Pastor Tim Callum referred to John's talk for the next three weeks. As others attested, that kind of response to one of John's talks was not uncommon.

One writer noted that even the "gravel in his voice as the disease restrict[ed] his vocal cords" contributed something to John's message as he pointed others toward the world's only proclaimer of ultimate truth, Jesus the Christ, who was *not* to be found in the grave. As the Apostle Paul wrote two thousand years ago, He has been *"declared the*

---

3 J. Rickard (Feb. 19, 2008), "Siege of Calais, 23-26 May 1940," *www.historyofwar.org/articles/siege_calais_1940.html*, accessed Jun. 8, 2020; Michael Glover, *The fight for the channel ports: Calais to Brest 1940: a study in confusion* (L. Cooper in association with Secker and Warburg: London, 1985) [emphasis in original].

4 E-mail, Glenn Draper to author, "Re: When John became headmaster," Jan. 18, 2020.

Son of God with power by the resurrection from the dead" (Romans 1:4). And without the resurrection, as John said at his home church, Eastwood Presbyterian, in April 2018, we may as well all go home. But the resurrection, Jesus coming out of the grave, "That's a game-changer." He exhorted his believing listeners, especially the young adults, to focus on the "inner man" of 2 Corinthians 4:16 which—guaranteed by Christ's resurrection—will one day be renewed in absolute perfection.[5]

[Note: Portions of this chapter were published online by *The Aquila Report*, Jul. 11, 2019.]

5 Marty Schoenleber, Jr., "Reflections of a Dying Christian," *ChosenRebel's Blog*, May 3, 2018; "John Geiger[:] Reflections of a Dying Christian," Apr. 15, 2018, Eastwood Presbyterian Church sermons, available at www.eastwoodchurch.org (accessed Jul. 6, 2019) (or on Google, search for "John Geiger, Reflections of a Dying Christian").

16

The Band of Brothers in Normandy

As previously stated, John and Dawn made a number of trips to Europe, including several with Eastwood graduating seniors. As part of the senior class excursions, they visited the Normandy beaches, including Omaha Beach, one of the two beaches where U.S. forces went ashore on June 6, 1944, to achieve a toehold on the European continent. The amphibious assault, part of Operation Overlord, was the first and all-important step toward the liberation of northwest Europe and the eventual defeat of the German military.[1]

The last time all the Geiger brothers had done something *big* together had been in 1997 when they joined their father, Robert, for a halibut fishing expedition to Alaska. Since then, they had talked about another excursion, possibly to the Normandy beaches, but plans never came to fruition. After their father died in 2015, the brothers again talked about a trip together, but still nothing developed. With John's diagnosis in the

1 While it detracts nothing from the accomplishments of those brave men who assaulted the Normandy beaches, Americans have tended to forget that roughly two-thirds of the German ground forces fought the Soviet Army on the Eastern Front.

summer of 2017, they all knew their trip-clock was ticking. John knew his four brothers had never seen the assault beaches or surrounding area. They had talked of going there for years even though not all of them were military history-minded or particularly interested in D-Day or World War Two. As a boy, John had enjoyed reading about the DC Comics character from that war, "Sgt. Frank Rock," who first appeared in 1959 and remained popular for the next thirty years. Fiction aside, the historical record of brotherhood, endurance, valor, and sacrifice exhibited in Normandy seemed appropriate for the Geigers, especially given the likelihood of it being the last gathering place for all five brothers. The setting could hardly help but make their time together the more memorable. When, in the summer of 2018, John's oldest brother, Bruce, and his wife, Linda, visited the family in Montgomery, John broached the subject again. This time, Bruce, Steve, Paul, and Greg were all in, and John quickly made arrangements for them to link up in Paris during the last week in September. It was to be just the brothers, hence the moniker, the *Band of Brothers.*

David and Kathryn Lohnes

A longtime missionary family, the Lohneses, were key figures in the planning for the Band of Brothers' Normandy tour. The Lohneses served a small non-denominational mission church in a town outside Paris. An ordained minister of the Gospel, David preached the Bible in French each Lord's day to a small but faithful congregation. Kathryn has supported him in the ministry since their arrival in 1981. In his free time, David became very familiar with the local history during World War Two, and for years he guided the Eastwood seniors through the sites of Normandy. He graciously accepted John's offer to lead the brothers' tour, revisiting many of the familiar wartime sites as well as adding several new ones that John had never seen with his students.

John's four brothers all lived in Visalia, California, so it was convenient for them to fly together out of Los Angeles International (LAX) airport (unlike John in 1987—see Chapter 6—they made sure NOT to park in the Delta employees' parking garage!) Their overnight, nonstop, flight arrived at Paris on September 26. Meanwhile, from Atlanta, John flew *alone* and was met in Paris by the Lohneses. After linking up with Bruce, Steve, Paul, and Greg, David drove the group to his home where the Geigers stayed for two of their four nights in France. During this part of the trip, in fact, for four of the five weeks he was away from Alabama, John suffered severe chills nightly, which soaked his tee-shirt. Hallucinations accompanied the chills. Several months later, John recalled there were times he felt something akin to a partial out-of-body experience. He actually believed he was dying. All of that was indicative of how badly he felt during much of the time he was alone. But when he was with the others, John managed to get by. David Lohnes wrote that "like a true soldier, he gave every ounce of effort to push through the obstacles and make this an unforgettable, life-changing experience."

Reminders of Sacrifice and Love

Over the course of the next three days, they visited several well-known sites from June 6th, 1944: the town of Sainte-Mère-Église—the first French town to be liberated by the Allies—and where the parachute of a paratrooper, Private John Steele, was caught on the church's bell tower, immortalized by Cornelius Ryan in his epic work, *The Longest Day*; La Pointe du Hoc, where U.S. Army Rangers fought their way up a one-hundred foot cliff to neutralize German guns that Allied intelligence assessed to be there, threatening the Allied landings on both the Utah and Omaha beaches;[2] and, at Arromanches-les-Bains, they visited one of the artificial harbors known as *Mulberries* that allowed for supplying the assault force once it was ashore. They also found time to see the famous cathedral at Bayeux, and they spent two nights at the Churchill Hotel there.

One of the lesser known places they visited was the German Military Cemetery at La Cambe. John had never been there before and it was especially sobering to see the rough-cut crosses of black granite that marked each soldier's well-kept grave, in stark contrast with the lush, green grass all around. The German cemetery's headstones also contrasted with the white stones of the American Military Cemetery at Colleville-sur-Mer, overlooking Omaha Beach. It was at one of the cemeteries, or perhaps

2 Unknown to the assault team, the Germans had moved the guns.

both, where the brothers found themselves reflecting that their own sons were about the same age as so many of the young men whose graves lay silently before them. One D-Day veteran of Pointe du Hoc—where 135 of 225 Rangers perished—expressed, "These men live in your memory. . . . Their personalities are frozen, they never develop." He continued, with palpable emotion, assessing the human cost of war: "All of their futures—gone. . . . All of their futures—gone." As John recalled, it was not hard to imagine that your own son could have been buried there. John had no doubt it was a good, and humbling, experience for all five of the brothers. During their stops in Normandy, the brothers took turns pushing John in his wheelchair, another sobering but also poignant opportunity for each one to demonstrate love for his dying brother.

Greg and Paul, the two youngest brothers, pulled more than their share of wheelchair duty. Although unforeseen, Greg found that duty to be a blessing; it helped him to reflect on John's love for him and for Christ. In a way that his older brothers were unable to experience to the same degree because of their years, Greg—who was five years younger than John—had seen and experienced John's early spiritual vitality and growth the most closely, and he had been at a very receptive age as a young teen. One particular incident Greg remembered and that the Lord used in his own spiritual development was when John went off by himself for a couple of days to pray through an important decision. In a manner unplanned by anyone beforehand, pushing John's wheelchair at sites where men had exhibited courage and sacrifice allowed each of the brothers to share his own unique remembrances of his relationship with John.

In the aftermath of their five days together in France, John's four brothers decided to commit to a regular gathering. As of the spring of 2019, Bruce, Steve, Paul, and Greg met once a month at some Visalia restaurant or pub to help maintain the brotherly affections the trip with John had allowed them to recapture. As John exhorted them over the phone in early March, shortly before Steve and his wife (Diana) moved to another state, "You'll need to work hard to be together" on a regular basis. John also encouraged his brothers to take advantage of the Lohneses' situation in France and their openness to visitors; perhaps they might bring their wives over at some point.

17

Last Trip Overseas

"Every once in a while, you get a real clear picture
[of God's will]. This trip was a clear picture."
– John Geiger, Jan. 2019

Background to the trip

Since the early 1990s, John and Dawn had visited Europe many times and spent two years in Russia not long after the Soviet Union's demise. Early in 2018, before the annual Eastwood senior class trip to Europe, a former Eastwood pastoral-intern-turned-church-planter invited John to Germany as a guest speaker at his church's retreat in the fall. Rev. Stephen Spanjer and the Geigers had known each other from Stephen's time at Eastwood when he was single. Soren Geiger interned with Stephen for six months after he graduated from high school. Several years later when Stephen married a daughter of Eastwood Presbyterian Church, Laura Goehring, his connection with his former church family grew even closer. With Stephen's request for John to come and speak on the topic of the dying Christian's hope of eternity, the Geigers made tentative plans for the late October retreat in the Black Forest region of southwest Germany, near the French and Swiss borders.

So far, John was planning two trips to Europe, one in late September with his brothers and another in late October. Then, a friend, Imran, unexpectedly called from Pakistan. In 2002, the Geigers had sponsored a Pakistan Air Force family during the husband's one year school assignment at Maxwell Air Force Base. Imran had enjoyed his time in Alabama, including hunting and fishing—activities John had enjoyed as a young man in California. Imran and his wife, Uzma, had three children about the same ages as the Geigers', and the two families had remained in contact, although not closely. Imran's older son had learned of John's ALS diagnosis on Facebook, and when he told his father, Imran called John to see how he was doing. As they talked, Imran mentioned that their daughter was to be married in October, in Pakistan. Already planning to be in Normandy barely a week before the wedding, John saw an opportunity to again demonstrate love for a family with whom he and Dawn had spent much time fifteen years earlier. John took the perhaps unorthodox step—while on the phone with Imran—of inviting himself to the wedding. Surprised, Imran was even more delighted that his American friend would be willing to come to his daughter's wedding, which was to be in Lahore. John, Dawn, and Nolin began planning a visit to Pakistan (only John was to be in Normandy).

With Normandy in late September, the wedding in Pakistan on October 6th, and a church retreat in Germany later in the month, John began thinking of the possibility of a *single* trip overseas, rather than two, if both health and family finances allowed. They had about three weeks in between the wedding and the church retreat. From their time in Russia in the early 1990s, the Geigers had a Russian friend who had done very well in business and lived part of the year in Barcelona, Spain. He invited John's family to spend time with him there, which was planned to be as restful as possible for John after the busy time in France and Pakistan.

At about the same time as Barcelona entered the picture, several former Eastwood students from Poland invited John to visit them as well. If their former headmaster was going to be in Germany, surely he must include Poland in his itinerary! Almost ten Polish students had attended Eastwood Christian School over the years, and three of them—including twins, Szon and Tim Tomkiewicz (Class of 2017), who had lived with the Geigers—took the initiative to organize a picnic near Warsaw.

John called them "my special Polish sons." With Dawn needing to return home to Alabama after the wedding (she still taught at ECS), the Geigers planned for John and Nolin to fly from Pakistan to France, then Poland, then on to Spain.

Amazingly, with the addition of Warsaw, their itinerary was not quite complete. John and Nolin were to manage a short stay at Basel, Switzerland, just prior to the church retreat, the location of which was not far away, perhaps an hour or so by car from Basel. But when the time came in late September for John to depart the United States, he was feeling poorly. Actually, he was feeling horrible. During four of the five weeks he was away from home, at nighttime John was to suffer from a combination of cold sweats, fever, and hallucinations. As John, Dawn, and Nolin affirmed especially after their return home, it clearly had been God's will for John to go on this trip. The reason was simple. Had the family, or John's doctor, known just how sick John was at the time, any trip whatsoever would have been ruled out. But it was not until December, about six weeks after John returned home, that it became evident he had been suffering from a blood disorder for several months and not merely from the symptoms of ALS. But during daytime activities, when he was with others and seeking to minister to them in some way—John experienced the Lord's kindness and compassion enabling him to engage well enough with those he was with.

Pakistan

Following the time with his brothers in France, John flew into Istanbul, Turkey, where he linked up with Dawn and Nolin who arrived from Montgomery, Alabama. They flew together into Lahore, Pakistan, arriving at 4am on the day before the wedding. On the day of the wedding, after a tour of Lahore in the morning, the Geigers were driven to the military base where the wedding was to be held. But, inexplicably, the security personnel were not satisfied with their documentation and delayed the family's entry to the base. By the time the Geigers finally were allowed to proceed, the ceremony was over and the reception was nearing its completion. John had hoped to remain anonymous and blend into the crowd, but after the lengthy delay the Geigers were treated with a police escort that could hardly remain unnoticed by the reception's roughly seven hundred celebrants. While they only had twenty minutes at the reception, as John recollected, it was enough for Imran's family to know that "we love you." Their driver, Naseem, playfully referred to the few minutes the Geigers had at the reception, saying, "This is our rendition of Pakistani fast food!" The day after the wedding, the Geigers enjoyed visiting with Imran and Uzma at their home, where they also reconnected with another Pakistani family they had known from Maxwell Air Force Base some years earlier. On Monday morning, the day of their departure, Nolin played a round of golf at the course next to the resort area where his family had been staying. That afternoon, the three of them attended an informal flag-lowering event at the (historically, often tense) Pakistani-Indian border, in which the soldiers of both countries cheered wildly for their nation's flag in a manner akin, as Dawn recalled, to a football game back home in Alabama (the cultural significance of which John now understood; see Chapter 7)!

Departing that evening from Lahore, the Geigers flew into Istanbul where Dawn parted from John and Nolin for her trip home. Seeking to provide a dose of counsel and comfort to her younger son who was staying with John for the remainder of the trip, she gently reminded Nolin that only God knows the number of your dad's days, and no one knows who will be with him when that time comes. While in the moment Nolin seemed to receive her words with more alarm than comfort, over the next three weeks he proved himself a capable translator, manservant, and Scripture reader for his father. In any case, Dawn's men continued on to Paris—where they stayed for several days of rest with the Lohneses—then on to Warsaw, while she returned home and to teaching.

While at the Istanbul airport, John spent a good while in the wheelchair waiting area with other passengers. He ended up next to a man from Belgium who had been through a rough couple of years. The man intended to return home and "find some spiritual roots." John engaged him in conversation:

> I told him I have had a rough couple of years. I mentioned all the gurus of truth (Confucius, Buddha, Aristotle, Mohammed)

> are in their grave and so are their perspectives. Jesus Christ is the one proclaimer of truth who rose from the dead and now proclaims truth that all men can use to guide their lives. His face lit up with a smile. "Thank you, I needed to hear this." . . . My wheelchair showed up and I was whisked away only to catch his name, Bruno.[1]

Poland

When John talked about the whole trip several months later, he reflected that Poland may have been the most interesting in one sense. There, unlike his other stops, he saw the full spiritual spectrum from those who professed faith in Christ and believed the Bible to others who claimed to be atheists, agnostics, or secularists. John spoke twice, first at the picnic that his former students had arranged. All but one of the former Eastwood students, along with their families, attended, while the other was out of the country. The twins, Szon and Tim, had expected to be out of the country, but a passport problem kept them in Poland and allowed them to surprise the Geigers at the airport. The next day, which was the Lord's day, John had been invited to preach at a local church, which he was delighted to do. Another interesting aspect to his short time in Poland was that John's two talks there were the only ones for which a translator was provided—all his other speaking engagements were in English only. Overall, John felt the response he received there had been very encouraging, especially from some who claimed no faith at all. One of them told John, "I need to re-think my atheism." Later, John reflected, "They were drawn to the message of the Bible, they were attracted to it." And as he and Nolin were at the airport preparing to depart for Barcelona, the father of one of the Eastwood students showed up on a motorcycle and presented John with, of all things, an authentic cowboy hat—an unexpected and memorable capstone to their Warsaw visit.[2]

---

1 John E. Geiger, "With My Last Breath—International Tour," ca. late 2018.

2 One might be tempted to view the popularity of American cowboy hats as yet another small example of the spread of Western culture.

Spain

John remembered Barcelona as a time of rest, after the busyness of Warsaw. The Geigers' Russian friend was married and had two children, and they spent a lot of time talking about raising kids. John's friend and his wife sought to raise their children biblically, and John described his time with them as a very pastoral, discipleship-focused, visit. There was an American school in Barcelona, a preparatory school for international kids intending to come to the United States for college. Their Russian friend's nephew had attended a grade school in New York for several years. In 2018 he was studying at Barcelona's American school. One of John's fellow elders back home was a pediatrician who had just published a book on child rearing. When John returned home, he mailed his friend a copy of Dr. Den Trumbull's book, *Loving By Leading: A Parent's Guide to Raising Healthy and Responsible Children.*

One big irritation for Nolin, however, was the problem he had in finding high-calorie liquid meals for his dad's feeding tube. When they departed from the United States, John was still able to swallow, and so he could eat at least some food, but that changed by the time they got to Spain. After scouring numerous shops in the area, Nolin found one that sold a drink that appeared to be sufficiently high in calories. The proprietor seemed to affirm the number on the label as "calories," so Nolin bought a case. Only later did he and John learn that the "800" marking on the container did not indicate the calories. John had been surviving on fewer calories and nutrients than he should have been getting, a fact that frustrated Nolin and caused him to "double-down" on his efforts to find high calorie liquid products.

Switzerland and Germany

Flying from Barcelona on October 22, John and Nolin arrived at Basel, Switzerland, on the Rhine River just south of the German border. Consistent with John's "young at heart" spirit which so many Eastwood students had enjoyed over the years, he and Nolin spent two nights at a youth hostel in Basel and visited with several friends in the area, including Ellis Potter, one of John's teachers from L'Abri three decades earlier.

During this brief stay, John also had the opportunity to speak with about one hundred fifty students, many of them missionary kids from Europe and the United States, at a nearby boarding school, the Black Forest Academy. Some were happy young people, John recalled, but others had anger issues at being sent away from home for school, or were struggling in their faith and their relationship with God. Those who were willing to talk with John found a listening ear and heard something of the hope that God was not finished with them yet, and He meets with those who turn to Him even with a weak faith or a double-minded heart.

On the 24th, Stephen Spanjer linked up with John and Nolin and drove them south to the Alps for an excursion. It was there at a hotel in the town of Mürren, Switzerland, the three of them gazing at three famous peaks across the valley—known as the Eiger, the Monch, and the Jungfrau—that Stephen recalled John's comment as he unsuccessfully tried to swallow small spoonfuls of hot broth. John stopped, looked at Stephen, and said, "The breakdown of my body has been an act of worship," because he realized, as Stephen recalled, "how complex his body was as he loses one muscle after the other—all the things in his body that he took for granted he was now beginning to notice—you don't know what you have until it is gone—and it caused him to worship." John's much younger pastor-friend added, "Such was the man and I'll never forget that line."

After seeing the Alps—which included an "amazing hike" that Stephen took Nolin on—they drove across the border and into the Black Forest town of Todtnauberg, Germany, for the church retreat. John spoke four times during the three-day retreat, about his life, discipleship, and suffering. Stephen Spanjer wrote,

> It was a blessing for everyone. At first people from my church were shocked that I would ask this man to speak at our conference in his condition and found it all a little morbid at first. But by the end of the weekend people were in love with John and moved by his courage and faith. His name has come up so many times in our church since then and was even a massive comfort

> to one of our members in particular. The day after the retreat, [this member flew to Cyprus]. He had been having headaches during the retreat but thought it was just a migraine. He arrived in Cyprus and had terrible blurred vision and the headache was worse, so he went to the hospital and they immediately thought . . . [he was] suffering a stroke. Normally, he would have panicked, being so far from home and in such a life threatening situation, but he said, "I remembered John and thought, I'm ready to die if that is what the Lord wants." He told this to the nurse and she was a little shocked at his calmness and confidence. After a few days of testing it turned out to be Bell's Palsy and he returned to Germany.[3]

Following the Lord's day morning worship, for which John preached at the youth hostel where the retreat was held, Stephen drove John and Nolin through a snowstorm to the Spanjers' home in Badenweiler. The next day, Stephen took them to the airport at Basel for a sad goodbye.

Several months later, John recalled that prior to the trip, "All the time I had an urgency in my spirit . . . to go." During those five weeks from late September to the end of October, God gave John the energy to interact and talk with people in no less than *six* different countries—France, Pakistan, France (again), Poland, Spain, Switzerland, and Germany—despite his losing weight and experiencing vomiting, diarrhea, and choking. Those symptoms were in addition to the nighttime afflictions he suffered during most of the trip. On many nights, David's words in Psalm 63:6-7 must have applied to John as well: "*When I remember Thee on my bed, I meditate on Thee in the night watches, For Thou hast been my help, And in the shadow of Thy wings I sing for joy.*"

Early in 2019, John summed up the whole trip this way: "I saw the hand of God on this trip. . . . We all know that God oversees our lives, everything." The Lord provided the money to go, we received gifts

3 E-mail, Stephen Spanjer to author, "Re : your church retreat, fall 2018," Jan. 28, 2019.

unsolicited, and a nice Blue Cross insurance refund fell into place, he said. On the way to the airport, John told Dawn, "my body is telling me I'm an idiot to try this." But as he shared, "I had an urgency in my spirit . . . to go," an inner confidence that he was *supposed* to go. "Overall, we saw the Lord at work with Christians and non-Christians . . . and I made it, I'm back."

18

Last Year and Last Breath Blog

It was only after John had returned home to Alabama from his six-country marathon in late October 2018—having suffered terribly especially during many nights—that his doctors discovered he had been afflicted with a blood disorder, in addition to the symptoms of ALS. If the blood condition had been known beforehand, his doctors would never have allowed the trip. John's blood ailment, the symptoms of which were apparently masked by the ALS, probably came on between late August and mid-September.

In early December, John went to Montgomery's Jackson Hospital for further testing to try and determine why he was still feeling so badly. When the blood issue was identified and the staff told him he was to be admitted at the hospital, John was surprised. Despite all his athletic and outdoor adventures earlier in life, including his share of minor injuries, sixty-year-old John Geiger had never spent a night in any hospital (at least not since infancy). Thankfully, his stay was not long and he was able to remain at home for his last thirteen months in "the earthly tent."

Greg Teal Tuesdays

During this time, the Geiger home continued to be a popular venue for the visits of many friends and family members. One of John's former students, Greg Teal, who in 2008 returned to teach at ECS, became a regular Tuesday afternoon visitor at the Geigers'. After John's last senior class trip to Europe in the spring of 2018, Greg agreed to take on the trip planning duties for 2019 and beyond. Greg began meeting with John almost weekly, going over the maps of the cities the students were to visit and discussing the possible contingencies in each locale. (As John knew from experience, Greg needed to be prepared to jump out of a subway at a moment's notice to retrieve something a student had left behind and then be able to rejoin the group!)

After the senior trip in March 2019, Greg continued his Tuesday visits. By that time, John was using a recently-acquired motorized, faster and more maneuverable wheelchair for getting around the house as well as at church—and he was pretty good with it. Dawn noted that "grandpa on wheels" was quite popular with the little ones, Leo and Evelyn, who were very "chill" just riding around on John's lap—but whether they required a "seatbelt" as had once been the case when Soren was a toddler was unspecified (see Chapter 7)! John was excited to show Greg what he could do with his new wheels, too. He was good at finding the small things to get excited about, and perhaps even more so for the sake of others.

On some of Greg's visits, they rode the golf cart around "the hill" and visited the horses. When John was no longer able to speak, he'd use his iPad to type out what he wanted to say. John had written many songs over the years, and on one occasion he played one of his songs on his iPad for Greg. Greg sometimes brought his guitar and played it, which John, a guitarist himself, enjoyed. (John loved Bob Dylan's music, as Greg and others attested.) Sometimes they looked at old photographs or cooked, and on one occasion John "talked" Greg (on his iPad) through the meal's entire preparation. On another, Greg fed John through the feeding tube, with John's coaching. The Teals had moved into a new home in Verbena, north of Montgomery, and in June 2019 John and Dawn came up for a visit and dinner together.

Recollection: Eric and Mary Agnes (Geiger) Walker

Reared in Idaho and eastern Washington State, Eric Walker graduated from a classical Christian school in Spokane before heading to Hillsdale College in Michigan. On his second day on campus in 2012, he met Mary Agnes Geiger and her cousin, Megan Geiger (she was Greg's daughter and thus John's neice). They were new arrivals to the college, too. Although impressed with Mary Agnes from the start, Eric noted she liked history, poetry, and hipster music whereas he was more interested in volleyball and economics, so he didn't think he "had a chance" with her. More than a year passed before a student dinner event placed him at the same table with her. The conversation was an eye-opener to him, he confessed in 2020, as many of his assumptions about her thinking and interests had been incorrect. For instance, she revealed her shared love for the American West. *Who knew?*

Finally, early in 2015 he began pursuing her and soon realized he needed to talk with her father—whom he had never met. Eric had the chance over spring break when about fifteen of Mary Agnes's classmates came to Alabama and stayed in the family cabin at Lake Jordan; he was among them. Eric and John took off on a drive in his truck and stopped at a nearby gas station for a soft drink. While there at the station's convenience store, John engaged the man at the counter, whose story he knew, and asked about his family members whose names he also knew from prior conversations. Eric took note: "The man cares about people and puts in the effort to know what's going on with their lives." John's future son-in-law was put at ease.

Eric and Mary Agnes were married after both of them graduated from Hillsdale in 2016. They settled in Idaho. A year later, when they learned of John's diagnosis, they decided *immediately* to move to Montgomery (which they accomplished over New Year's week of 2018) in order to be near John and Dawn, Nolin, and—a year later when they moved back from Michigan—Soren and Virginia's family as well.

In their two years with the family before John's death, living on "the hill" within easy reach of the Geiger home, the Walkers observed and often appreciated firsthand John's excellence in the kitchen. Mary Agnes said her dad was a really good cook but that his niche was doing "the specialty meals." Especially when the Polish twins, Szon and Tim, came to live with John, Dawn, and Nolin, suddenly there were *three teen-aged males* in the house to feed. "Dad took over some of the meals . . . it brought him joy to cook," Mary Agnes recalled. Even after he could no longer eat, her dad continued much of the meal planning, and part of the household routine included making sure someone was available to help John in the kitchen. He'd have someone to taste-test each dish for him, and even without tasting it himself he knew when to add a couple more dashes to make it "spot-on, spice-wise," according to his daughter. Mary Agnes summed up: "He was very specific in the kitchen; this was when he was in a wheelchair, couldn't eat, barely talk." Later, those times in the kitchen with her dad brought back many good memories. Eric noted that Mary Agnes did much of the cooking with John—she was "his hands" for many meals in the Geiger home.

Eric also commented on how his father-in-law prepared the family so well for his death: "He told us *why* he was dying, *how* he was . . . going to [seek to] use his death, so well. . . . It felt like *a cause* we could get behind; the message that can be shared from John's death is *bigger* than John's death." When the time came, he and Mary Agnes agreed, it lessened the pain.

Reflections: Soren and Virginia (Lasseter) Geiger

Soren and Virginia Geiger were one of at least a dozen married couples who had attended ECS together. Soren graduated in 2008, Virginia in 2009; they married in 2013 following Soren's graduation from Hillsdale College where he remained working—it was an amazing opportunity—with the papers of Winston Churchill. In the latter half of 2019, after Soren, Virginia, and their young son, Leo, moved back to Montgomery—residing at the Carriage House on "the hill"—Virginia had greater opportunities to experience her father-in-law's precision and expertise in the kitchen. She recalled some of John's favorite dishes were vichyssoise, meatballs, and beef burgundy, and "he'd tell us what to do" using his own recipes—recall that by this time John had long since ceased being able to eat or even taste, and he "talked" mainly by iPad. John never looked at a recipe, Virginia said, he just remembered what he'd done before or tried something a little different. Her father-in-law introduced her to a lot of good food (see Appendix B).

In October 2016, Ruby Mae Geiger was born. She was Soren and Virginia's first child and John and Dawn's first grandchild. It was discovered hours after her birth that she had the serious heart condition AVSD, which effectively resulted in oxygenated blood being pumped back to her lungs instead of out to her body. She was 26 days old when she died in her parents' arms after suffering a cardiac arrest. Soren and Virginia were living in Michigan, and John, Dawn, and Nolin happened to be visiting when Ruby died. Soren and Virginia treasure the memories they have of John, Dawn, and Nolin holding and loving on Ruby Mae. On what would have been the day she turned three, John wrote on his blog: "As I grieved Ruby Mae's death a song was birthed. We all missed her. We focused on eternal truths from God. We knew she lived though her little body died. We watched the Holy Spirit comfort her parents. We looked forward to the return of Jesus and the end of death. These thoughts shaped the lyrics." (For other blog entries, see Appendix C.)

Last Breath Blog Ministry

Another part of John Geiger's ministry even in his last months was his *Last Breath Blog*, of which "*The Mucus Monster*" (Dec. 17, 2019) was a fine example:

> The beast, a wretched foe, goes for the throat, seeking to strangle its victim. Last Monday it crept into my bedroom, pounced on me, fastened its claws on my throat, and we began a five hour murderous battle. Visions of Beowulf and Grendel's gladiatorial wrestling match occupied my mind. I denied it victory several times. Weary, I entertained the possibility of defeat. Then, as if spooked, the Mucus Monster released its grip and fled. As it left I heard the slimy murderer hiss, "I shall return."
>
> Mucus (phlegm) is constantly swallowed by the average person. Due to ALS my swallowing is minimal and my ability to cough and clear my throat is practically nil. So, the mucus builds

and lodges in my air passage (I have dubbed this—The Mucus Monster). The effort to clear this and breathe is traumatic. It is a real battle.

During the five hour struggle my brain was still functioning well. A comforting thought kept going through my mind: "I am only gasping for air! I am only gasping for air! The important issues of life are settled."

I reminded myself I wasn't gasping for truth—"Jesus said to him, 'I am the way, and the truth, and the life. No one comes to the Father except through me."

I reminded myself I wasn't gasping for love—"This is love, not that we loved God but that He loved us and sent His Son [Jesus] as an atoning sacrifice."

I reminded myself I wasn't gasping for peace—"Peace I [Jesus] leave with you; my peace I give you. I do not give to you as the world gives. Do not let your hearts be troubled and do not be afraid."

I reminded myself I wasn't gasping for salvation—"And there is salvation in no one else, for there is no other name [Jesus] under heaven given among men by which we must be saved."

You see the controlling idea here? It is Jesus Christ.

Without Him, everything collapses. With Him, everything holds together.

After the Mucus Monster left, this Christmas hymn flooded into my spirit—"Come, Thou Long Expected Jesus." Notice the last two lines of the first verse:

Come, Thou long expected Jesus
Born to set Thy people free;
From our fears and sins release us,
Let us find our rest in Thee.
Israel's strength and consolation,
Hope of all the earth Thou art;
Dear desire of every nation,
Joy of every longing heart.

This "Dear desire of every nation, Joy of every longing heart" is better than air in my lungs. His real birth, His real death, His real resurrection, and His real return provide answers to mankind's questions, solutions to mankind's problems, and joys for mankind's longings.

I can't fathom a more treasured thought to grasp this Christmas. While there is air in our lungs, let us hold onto Him who is better than air.

Merry Christmas 'til my last breath, John[1]

Last Months, 2019

John continued attending worship services at his church, Eastwood Presbyterian, for as long as possible. In November, his close friend from Fresno State forty years earlier, Lawrence Kersten, drove from Dallas, Texas, to the Geigers' home for what was to be their last time together on this side of glory. Later, Lawrence commented that "even with his diminished motor movements, his mind was so vibrant and alert when I was there." Lawrence joined John and Dawn for worship. John continued to attend worship until the middle of December.

Knowing John as well as he did, Lawrence was well-positioned to highlight an important, but perhaps sometimes overlooked, aspect of John's ministry. Simply put, Lawrence knew well that it was John *and Dawn's* ministry. They were a team. John's consistent practice of reaching out to others was legendary, but his ability to do so also depended greatly on Dawn. As a case in point, Lawrence recalled the time—probably one of many with a similar outline—when the Polish twins who were coming to the United States as part of a sports ministry needed a place to stay. John told the ministry leader that if they could not find a host family for the twins, he would take them. As Lawrence remembered from John's mentioning the event, when John told Dawn that he had agreed to take in the two students, she asked for how long they would be staying with them. "John said he didn't know; maybe for a semester," Lawrence recalled.

1 John Geiger, *Last Breath Blog*, "The Mucus Monster," Dec. 17, 2019, at www.https//lastbreathblog.com, accessed Jun. 25, 2020.

When another student involved in the same ministry who was hosted in another state found out "how great it was to stay with John and Dawn," that student asked to be transferred to Montgomery and to stay with the Geigers. All three students ended up with the Geigers for an extended period. Lawrence wrote,

> The thing that struck me was how hospitable John and Dawn were. I could not imagine telling my wife that I have a teen from [a foreign country] who is going to be staying with us for an indeterminate amount of time. . . . I don't know many women who would be open to allowing teen males stay in their home for an indeterminate period of time, but I was glad to see that . . . Dawn was the ministry partner that was well suited for John.[2]

On another Lord's day late in the year, John saw the chance after the service to zip around the sanctuary in his wheelchair and to catch up with an ECS grad, Amelia Rhodes. She was there with a young man, her boyfriend, whom John wanted to meet. Knowing something of the relationship beforehand, John had been praying for them (which he typed out on his iPad). If one had not known of John's condition, one never could have figured it out from the way he engaged with others and continued to express such love and concern for them.

---

2 E-mail, Edward L. ("Lawrence") Kersten to author, "Re: Austin trip, 2008," Feb. 25, 2020. The incident discussed in the text occurred several years later than the subject line of the e-mail indicated (not 2008).

19

Reflections of Brotherhood: Bruce Stewart

Author's note: Several long-serving ECS faculty recalled that John had taken on the role of advising Eastwood seniors in preparing their graduation speeches; when Rhetoric was added to the curriculum as a requirement for seniors, the graduation speech was the focus of the class. I assumed therefore that John had advised even *the first* ECS graduate, Bruce Stewart, who finished in the spring of 2000 as the lone member of his class. In our interview together in December 2019, at Martha's Place in Montgomery, Bruce corrected me on this point and added much more.

Bruce noted that Eastwood Christian School began in 1996, one year before John Geiger assumed duties as the upper school humanities teacher. During Bruce's last three years there, John taught Bruce and the rest of the upper school students in several subjects, including logic and Bible. Bruce had little recollection of his relationship with "Mr. Geiger" during those years other than as a respected teacher, although he also remembered his instructor's ability to communicate things in a very unique way, especially with Bruce's age group.

Bruce *definitely* did not have the assistance of John Geiger with his senior speech. Readily acknowledging his tendency to procrastinate in those days, Bruce recalled that the night before graduation he busily jotted down his thoughts and a list of those he wanted to thank. It was not a recipe for success. Looking back almost twenty years later, Bruce felt certain it was because of his speech "being so poorly done" that John was asked to begin working with the seniors from then on. Bruce imagined certain parents—including his mom, Priscilla—a school board member—and others saying, "Hey, we've gotta do something different next year because we can't let this happen again." From that time through the spring of 2018 when John retired, ECS seniors' graduation speeches received the attention they deserved.

Bruce's nearest brother in age was Drew, who graduated the following year, 2001. Not only did Drew and his three fellow seniors have the advantage of John Geiger's considerable help with their speeches, Drew credited John's relationship and time spent with him—including outside the classroom—as playing no small part in leading him toward his career as a special education middle school teacher in Aubrey, Texas. As John had modeled with him, Drew's position allowed him to pursue highly supportive relationships with his students.

While Bruce and John's relationship was strictly that of student and teacher at first, several years later things changed dramatically for them. In 2007, Bruce married Johanna Lasseter, a daughter of another Eastwood family. Several years later, Soren Geiger—John and Dawn's oldest—married Virginia, Johanna's sister. An added link was that Clara, another Lasseter sister, shared the same birthdate as John Geiger, November 13. Each year, they playfully tried to be the first to wish "happy birthday" to the other. Because of Soren and Bruce's marriage to Lasseter sisters, as Bruce put it, "I started spending time around the Geiger family in a way that we had never done before." Instead of seeing Mr. Geiger as the teacher, theologian, and logic instructor, Bruce experienced a blossoming friendship with a much older man for perhaps the first time outside of his own immediate family.

It was "a friendship, more of a brotherhood," Bruce explained. John communicated to him something he had not experienced before, an older man saying, essentially: "I have as much to gain from you as you have to potentially gain from me." Not many men, Bruce observed, seemed willing to communicate that to a much younger man, desiring friendship and to learn from them, even to be accountable to them. Over the years, Bruce had plenty of opportunities to observe John as a husband, father, and also a grandfather, which he described, simply, as "very special."

In 2019, Bruce recalled a recent Sunday School study from the Book of Numbers, the section in which the spies entered Canaan and brought back their report. Bible readers will recall that ten of the twelve spies faltered; only Joshua and Caleb returned with words of faith, anticipating victory over the enemies of God. Reflecting whether Joshua and Caleb's greater legacy was one of faith and obedience more so than military conquest, Bruce likened John's life to the biblical narrative. From the younger man's perspective, John is a man coming to the end of his life, a man "who is leaving a legacy of obedience and a legacy of faithfulness," in the same mold as Joshua and Caleb, one who has lived out the words he has professed to so many over the years. Bruce concluded by saying that if you didn't know that John was suffering from ALS, and you were trying to get a feel for this guy based only on what he communicates (which by late 2019 was strictly electronic, using his iPad), you would never know that he was about to meet the Lord. Even now, John's focus is not on himself, not on his condition, but on others, and on Christ, the true warrior-king—as Joshua and Caleb well knew.

> [Note: Eighteen days after Bruce Stewart offered these thoughts, John entered into the presence of the Lord Jesus Christ, on January 7, 2020.]

20

Last Breath

"John died last night about 11pm. . . .

As for me, I shall behold your face in righteousness; when I awake, I shall be satisfied with your likeness.—Psalm 17:15."

– Pastor Bart Lester to Eastwood's elders,
5:55am, Jan. 8, 2020

As late as the Christmas holidays, 2019, the Geigers continued to host friends who came by to see them on "the hill." John's decline in recent weeks had been noticeable. Yet somehow he was still capable, as David Miller put it, of saying "more in one phrase than anyone else." David referred to John and Dawn having him over for dinner in mid-to-late December. Unable to speak for some months by that time, John took the opportunity to type a short message on his iPad to his friend and longtime teacher: "It was a huge risk I took in hiring you, but it paid off." It was another example of John's unique blend of honesty and humor, David recalled. Fourteen years earlier, the week before school started, David was one year out of Rhodes College in Memphis, Tennessee, with a bachelor's degree in Biology supplemented with an almost-minor in the Classics (including Latin). He was working on a farm near Verbena, Alabama, when a friend told him he should talk with John Geiger. He did so, and John hired him on the spot to teach one Latin class he still needed to fill. David began on the following Monday. A year later, in 2006, David transitioned to full-time teaching in Latin and the sciences.

Their relationship deepened when, in 2012, David joined the senior trip to Europe. In the evenings, he, John, and the other chaperones often relaxed together in the hotel lobby after a hectic day of counting students, catching subways, and experiencing cultural sites. As astute observers of the Coronavirus Quarantine of 2020 noted, "third places"—certain venues other than one's home or work—are socially important, providing opportunities for people to connect with one another in ways that promote mental stability while deepening friendships. For David and John, it was those settings in the evenings that let "different conversations happen," even a different mood, than previously had been the norm for them, allowing their friendship to blossom. Among other things, David recalled John sharing in some of those conversations his vision for the school or things God was doing in the lives of students. A year later, on the Paris Metro *"I'll find you" trip* (see Chapter 12), David had been struck with the thought: "You never knew what John was doing, but once you knew him you had faith that he'd get it done." Even in uncertain situations—including John's ALS diagnosis four years later—David enjoyed a calm assurance that his friend and mentor somehow was going to "get it done," which for John meant continuing to speak into people's lives, pointing them to Christ, for as long as possible.

On New Year's day, John was well enough to be wheeled next door to the Nolins' for a family gathering. But that night was the first of the really bad nights, Dawn recalled. It was clear John's earthly tent had begun tearing down. In the Apostle Paul's words, it was soon to be replaced with "a house not made with hands, eternal in the heavens"—which occurred at about 11pm on the 7th of January. Given John's circumstances due to ALS, his last words of faith in Jesus and comfort to family and friends—rather than spoken on his deathbed—had been expressed some days earlier as he typed out final messages to many on his iPad; each message to be long-treasured by the recipient. On the Lord's day afternoon following John's death, an estimated six to seven hundred family members, friends from church and school—including former students, teachers, and colleagues—and others from the wide-ranging connections that John and Dawn had enjoyed over many years of engaging for the sake of the gospel, gathered at Eastwood Presbyterian Church to honor John's memory and to worship Christ. (The number in attendance at John's memorial approximated that from the special event held two years earlier, *A Knight to Celebrate*, also at Eastwood.)

The Geigers' longtime friends, David and Kathryn Lohnes, who were in the United States (visiting from France) at the time of John's death, attended. David gave the main address. About six months earlier, Dawn had called and invited David to speak at John's memorial service. John, Dawn, and the entire family had been in agreement. Later, John wrote David and explained why he had asked him to speak: "I asked you because you know me so well, because you will tell the truth, and because you will talk more about Jesus than you will about me."

Later in 2020, Pastor Lohnes wrote of his preparation for the inevitable event:

> This, then, became my 3-fold mandate as I began to pray and prepare for that day. I wanted it to be known, and proudly so, that John Geiger, counted me among his intimate friends, as well as a friend of his family. I wanted to tell the truth about the horrors of death contrasted with the undeniable hope of the resurrection. I wanted to talk a little about John, but mostly about John's Risen Lord and Savior, Jesus-Christ. He would often say to me, "David, there is something bigger than death in this room! It's the person of the *living,* risen, Christ who has eradicated once and for all the eternal, permanent sting of death and has promised us the hope of eternal life. Death is an enemy, and it is a formidable one, and it will have its way with . . . all of us, but now . . . there is nothing to fear."[1]

On the afternoon of January 12, 2020, at Eastwood Presbyterian Church, David Lohnes gave that message, honoring his friend—but even

1 E-mail, David V. Lohnes to author, "John's Funeral Service," Jun. 30, 2020.

more importantly—pointing upwards of seven hundred in attendance to the resurrected Lord Jesus Christ, whom John loved and served. From his conversations with John since the diagnosis in 2017, David shared with the gathering:

> Every conversation I had with John these past 2 years (and there were many), every question I asked him about suffering, fear, loss, disappointment, disease, unfulfilled dreams, separation, physical limitations and death . . . all ended the same way—with these two words; Jesus and Hope! John's last words to me on this earth were spoken as we parted ways in [October] 2018 at the Charles de Gaulle Airport in France. . . . "Faithfulness to Jesus is worth it. It is not always easy, in fact sometimes it seems impossibly hard, but it's always worth it. Remain faithful to Jesus, David, and I'll meet you at the finish line!"[2]

In closing, two recollections from members of the ECS community seemed to capture a large part of the essence of John Edwin Geiger's life, heart, service, and faithfulness to Christ: one from a graduate in the middle years of John's tenure, the other from a teacher who served shoulder to shoulder with him for almost as long as anyone else. The graduate's words have been echoed by others in conversations, e-mails, and text messages over the course of preparing this work:

> From dressing up for the Olympic Field Games in [lower] school to the weekly chapels in upper school to Applied Theology and senior speeches, Mr. Geiger was the cornerstone of my education. He fostered a holistic learning environment that brought together all kinds of people. [He] taught us how to think for ourselves and communicate our beliefs to others. He greatly influenced my love of history and literature—something that shaped me into the person I am today.[3]

2 E-mail, Lohnes to author, Jun. 30, 2020.

3 E-mail, Ansley K. Markwell to author, "Re: JG Bio," Jul. 12, 2020.

Ansley Markwell, from the Class of 2012, was certain that "countless other 'Eastwoodians'" could say the same.

Following seven years of teaching 3rd grade at ECS and the next ten years serving as the lower school principal, Susan Gaines graciously agreed to serve as the interim head of the school when John retired in the spring of 2018. Midway through her two years' service in that important leadership role, she shared these thoughts regarding her friend, mentor, and former boss, which—like Ansley Markwell's—have been echoed by others:

> The world that I live in . . . is a more Christ-focused place . . . because God chose to place John Geiger here and to use him. And to God be the glory; that's what it's all about. This world is not about us. John knows that. It's about Him. It's a life well-lived. [John] is a man that I am absolutely positive when he stands before the Lord, He will say, 'Well done, My good and faithful servant.'[4]

Faithful . . . to his last breath.
FINI

4 Interview, Susan H. Gaines with author, Montgomery, Ala., Feb. 8, 2019.

Appendix A

John's Songs

I Forgive You (The Playground Song)

G EM C D
If someone hurts you what do you do?
If someone hurts you what do you do?
G
Do you hurt them right back?
C
No, No, No.
Do you hurt them right back?
No, No, No.
G D7 G
I forgive you.
I forgive you.

If someone hits you what do you do?
If someone hits you what do you do?
Do you hit them right back?
No, No, No.
Do you hit them right back?
No, No, No.
I forgive you.
I forgive you.

If someone pushes you what do you do?
If someone pushes you what do you do?
Do you push them right back?
No, No, No.
Do you push them right back?
No, No, No.
I forgive you.
I forgive you.

If someone's nice to you what do you do?
If someone's nice to you what do you do?
Are you nice right back?
Yes, Yes, Yes.
Are you nice right back?
Yes, Yes, Yes.
I love you.
I love you.

Psalm 139

[*Note from John:* On August 2, 1984, I was sitting on a porch in Bangalore, India. I was having a wonderful time in the Scriptures with our Lord. This tune popped into my head as I read Psalm 139. I was amazed at God's ability to be everywhere and know everything and still love me and want to help me.]

G Bm C D
If I ascend to heaven—You're there
Em G C D
To flee from thy presence—Your Spirit never leaves
G Bm C D
If I make my bed in Sheol—You're there
Em G C D
To fly with wings of the dawn still there you will lead

```
G   Bm   C                    D
O Lord search and know my heart
G   Bm   C              D
O Lord try my anxious thoughts
      Em            Bm
And see if my life's hurtful
      C                         D
And lead me in the everlasting way
```

If I'm deep under the ocean—You're there
Thy right hand will lay hold of me and lead me on my way
If I cover from the blinding light—You're there
Darkness cannot hide me for night is just like day
O Lord search and know my heart
O Lord try my anxious thoughts
And see if my life's hurtful
And lead me in the everlasting way

```
      Em                Bm
How precious are thy thoughts to me
      C        D
How vast is the sum of them
   Em              Bm
If I should try and count them
      C                                D
They would outnumber the sands of the sea
```

O Lord search and know my heart
O Lord try my anxious thoughts
And see if my life's hurtful
And lead me in the everlasting way

Fruit of the Spirit

Love, joy, peace
these are fruit
They have no earthly branch or root
The Spirit of God
He gives us all His good fruit

Patience, kindness
these are fruit
They have no earthly branch or root
The Spirit of God
He gives us all His good fruit

If you want to have this fruit
You must have the Spirit too
The Spirit must live in you
The Spirit must live in you

Goodness, faithfulness are fruit
They have no earthly branch or root
The Spirit of God
He gives us all His good fruit

Gentleness is a fruit
It has no earthly branch or root
The Spirit of God
He gives us all His good fruit

Self-control is a fruit
It has no earthly branch or root
The Spirit of God
He gives us all His good fruit

If you want to have this fruit
You must have the Spirit too
The Spirit must live in you
The Spirit must live in you

Appendix B

John's Recipes

Bootleg Salad

The Salad:

Field greens
Pickled okra
Greek olives
Feta cheese
Capers and Caper berries (optional)
Grape tomatoes (optional)

The Dressing:

- ¾ c. light olive oil
- ¼ c. fresh-squeezed lemon juice
- pressed garlic cloves (2 or 3)
- capers (a bit of the juice is fine as well)
- 1 tsp. salt and pepper or Greek Seasoning. We use Cavender's.
- sugar to taste (about 1 T.)

Slowly add lemon juice to olive oil according to your own taste. The amounts are proportions depending on how much dressing you want to mix up at once. The sugar is just to diffuse the tartness. You can see that the dressing is mixed according to taste. The ingredients are listed, now you have to experiment a bit to suit your palate. Also, the longer the dressing sits, the better it gets.

The dressing saves well and is excellent as a marinade for fish prior to grilling or boiling.

> [Note: We call it Bootleg Salad because it is patterned after the Field Greens Salad at the old Montgomery Brewing Co. in downtown Montgomery. I don't know how many orders we consumed before John felt like he had our own "little brown jug of dressing" perfected.]

Vichyssoise

Makes about 8 cups (we usually double or triple the recipe)

In a large soup pot:

Mince and sauté in 3 tablespoons of butter:
- 3 medium-sized leeks: white part only
- 1 or 2 medium-sized onions

Add:
- 4 cups chicken broth (or stock)

Pare, slice very fine (grating is easiest) and add:
- 4 medium-sized potatoes (to thicken consistency)

Add:
- 1/4 teaspoon of black pepper
- Salt to taste

Simmer the broth with the vegetables for about 45 minutes or until the potatoes are tender. Stir frequently to avoid sticking. The consistency of the soup is important. It should not be too watery and yet not too thick so the soup looks like lava bubbling. The true consistency is not known until the potatoes have tenderized; this takes about 30 minutes. At that point, if the soup is too thick, add more broth. If it is too thin, you have two options. You can add another grated potato (but you must cook the soup longer to tenderize the new shavings) or you can add a tablespoon of cornstarch mixed in a half cup of cold broth.

When the mixture is ready, add:
- 1 to 2 cups of half and half or cream.

Serve:

You can serve it as is or garnish the top of each bowl of soup with a bit of chopped chives (or the green part of a regular green onion). You could also add a sliver of another color, say, a red or orange bell pepper.

Some people like to cool the mixture and put it in a blender before adding the cream. We like to eat it hot.

Boeuff Bourguignon

In a large pot:
Cut and fry gently:
- 6 slices of bacon

Remove bacon and brown carefully and rapidly in bacon fat and a bit of olive oil:
- 6 pounds of good stewing beef

Add and deglaze the bottom of the pot:
- 3 or 4 cups of burgundy or dry red wine
- 2 cups of beef broth

Add and simmer until beef is tender:
- 2 tablespoons tomato paste
- 3 cloves of crushed garlic
- ½ teaspoon thyme
- 1 bay leaf
- Salt to taste
- Cooked bacon

Add and let simmer 20 minutes:
- 1 pound mushrooms browned in butter
- 2 or 3 chopped onions browned in butter

Thicken with a roux of ½ cup of flour browned in ½ cup of butter

Appendix C

From the Blog

December 29, 2018
"Dawn's Reflections on a Tree"

This year our Christmas tree almost wasn't a Christmas tree. The last on the lot, we got it for a steal. Free, that is. Good things come to those who wait (or procrastinate as the case may be.) I think the message from the generous folks at Boy Scouts of America went something like this: "It's 12 feet tall and six feet wide. If they can haul it off, they can have it." We hauled it off within the hour.

Remember how Charlie Brown rescued the overlooked tree that was too small and flimsy? Well, we rescued the equivalent of its arboreal doppelganger. Too tall and too wide, it was destined to be bonfire fuel before ever being adorned with lights and tinsel. But with some serious pruning with loppers and chainsaw, we managed to get it inside where the carols were playing and the wassail was brewing. Thanks Nolin (son) and Eric (son-in-law) and Chad (good friend) for adding muscle to our Christmas spirit so that this tree could find our home.

Destined for destruction, redeemed, pruned, adorned, and given the purpose of shining brightly through the season of long, dark nights—there's a lesson in that. Like our spruce, we long to be brought in from the cold and given a home. I like analogies.

Speaking of which, John was sitting and looking at our big tree (which literally fills up a good portion of the room) and he mused,

"Our year has been a lot like that tree. We too have had gifts piled up around us. We too have had the opportunity to shine light in places we've never visited. We could have felt cold and rejected, but instead we are surrounded with love and good friends and precious family." Good thoughts on paper; helpful thoughts to read and ponder. But if you could have heard him say it, you may have noted the stark contrast between his message and his experience. Speaking becomes more and more difficult with each passing week. Forming the words and making himself understood takes a lot of effort (and patience) on his part. Likewise, listening carefully and decoding takes a lot of effort (and patience) on our part. But when we get past the confusion, we find treasures like the one about the tree. His perspective is one of blessing, not loss, and it's worth the effort it takes to share it with others.

When I think about it, John himself is a lot like our Christmas tree (although he is beginning to look a little more like Charlie Brown's.) So before we all begin dismantling the evergreens that grace our living rooms, I'd like to conclude with the old German ode to the Christmas tree as my way of saying thanks, John, for being steadfast in every season.

O Christmas tree, O Christmas tree,
Thy leaves are so unchanging;
Not only green when summer's here,
But also when it's cold and drear.
O Christmas tree, O Christmas tree
Thy leaves are so unchanging.

January 2, 2019
An excerpt from "A Welcome Search"

"Search me, O God, and know my heart; Try me, and know my anxious thoughts; And see if there is any wicked way in me, And lead me in the way everlasting."

King David of Israel invited God to diagnose any hidden spiritual illness festering in his soul. This is a courageous prayer. This is a suitable prayer to start one's year. What a wonderful year 2019 would be if the infections of our soul's blood were exposed! They need to be treated with the blood of Christ.

January 13, 2019
An excerpt from "Skin, Bones, and a Little Bit of Muscle"

What now is important? Loving God and loving others. In the two great commandments we see what renews our inner man, what will last for eternity, and what is really important.

March 6, 2019
An excerpt from "Three Ships Passing in the Day"

Contentment is not found by reshaping life's external circumstances. Contentment comes by reshaping the life within.

April 16, 2019
"I Miss Eating"

I keep having this recurring daydream. I am at a mountain stream with a tin cup in my hand. I dip into the current and bring a refreshing drink of cool water to my lips. Deep draughts slowly roll down my throat. Over and over again I return the cup to the stream. Then my hand goes to a basket I had placed in the shallows. I pull out a pear and crush its icy pulp with my teeth. Four or five bites and it is gone. I reach down into the frigid basket and my fingers find a peach. I chuckle to myself over how good this is going to taste.

Such are the daydreams of those who eat via a feeding tube. No liquids or solids go through my mouth anymore. The good news is that my choking spells are seriously better; there is no longer anything to choke on. I still help in the kitchen by giving orders on how the meal for the family should be prepared. I know I have become a bit demanding of my sous-chefs (and I am guilty of watching too much of the Food Network), but I find great joy over watching my family enjoy meals. I vicariously dine with them. . . .

Lately, I have been pondering how the curse of sin and death was brought into this world through eating. Adam and Eve actualized their disobedience through consuming the forbidden fruit. What started in man's spirit was manifested through his body. Our physical ills have their source in a broken spirit. My ALS is a manifestation of the grand rebellion humans displayed against God. The beauty of our world was shattered through the pride of mankind. And so we all die . . .

But God, rich in mercy, did not leave us in this condition. When the Church celebrates Christ's resurrection this month, we recall Passion Week and the Last Supper.

And when he [Jesus] had given thanks, he broke it [the bread], and said, "This is my body, which is for you. Do this in remembrance of me." In the same way also he took the cup, after supper, saying, "This cup is the new covenant in my blood. Do this, as often as you drink it, in remembrance of me." (1 Corinthians 11:24-25)

The healing of man's condition is found in Christ. "By His stripes we are healed," said the prophet Isaiah. Jesus invites us into His life. We sacredly commune through our mouths with Christ. His body and blood are spiritually in us.

What did Jesus tell the Samaritan woman? "[W]hoever drinks of the water that I will give him will never be thirsty again. The water that I will give him will become in him a spring of water welling up to eternal life." And then during the Feast of Tabernacles,

On the last day of the feast, the great day, Jesus stood up and cried out, "If anyone thirsts, let him come to me and drink. Whoever believes in me, as the Scripture has said, 'Out of his heart will flow rivers of living water.'"

We really are being made into new creatures, ones that can dwell in the new heavens and the new earth. Allow me to finish by turning our thoughts to the Apostle John's revelation:

Then the angel showed me the river of the water of life, bright as crystal, flowing from the throne of God and of the Lamb through the middle of the street of the city; also, on either side of the river, the tree of life with its twelve kinds of fruit, yielding its fruit each month. The leaves of the tree were for the healing of the nations. . . . They will need no light of lamp or sun, for the Lord God will be their light, and they will reign forever and ever.

Everlasting water for the thirsty. Everlasting fruit for the hungry. Christ is everything and He offers everything.

And so, my friends, when you arrive in heaven, please come find me—I will be down by the river.

July 24, 2019
An excerpt from "The Sound of Silence"

My body is dying. My lungs are now functioning at 24%. Respiratory failure is what normally kills the ALS patient. But, I do not fear this valley of death for I am alive within and will live eternally. This is only by the grace, kindness, and sacrifice of Jesus. I can't keep silent about that.

October 14, 2019
"Heard about the Herd?"

"Horses are herd animals," my daughter said recently explaining her purchase of the second horse in six months. I had to admit the two did look happy and natural out there in the pasture. So now Winona and Trigger are rarely seen apart; they are a herd.

In 2016 several upper school boys at Eastwood were dubbed The Nerd Herd. The Nerd Herd spent as much school time together as they could. You could see them sitting in the hallways, hear them talking about video games or soccer, or watch them building a Herd Hut in the woods behind the school. The Hut was quite impressive—stone-paved entrance, couch, roof—all items found in the woods. It was the envy and talk of all the younger boys. The nerds enjoyed each other and one couldn't help but enjoy them enjoying each other. They were a herd.

My daughter and family moved from Idaho to Montgomery when they heard of my ALS diagnosis. They live 100 yards behind Dawn and me. My oldest son and family recently moved from Michigan. They live 30 yards behind me. He thought this was a good time for law school and to be near us. My youngest son sacrificially changed his college choices to a local school so he could continue to live with us—40 feet down the hall. My herd has gathered. I have a surprisingly deep joy in the midst of this chaos—laughter, teasing, preparing meals, grandchildren climbing, exploring, eating, throwing food, screaming, giggling—all part of the herd. I feel like I have been handed a gift from God. His kindness knows no bounds. My heart is a herd heart. Humans are herd creatures.

Then the LORD God said, "It is not good that the man should be alone; I will make him a helper suitable for him." We were created for fellowship. This should not surprise us; we were made in the image of the triune God—Father, Son, and Holy Spirit. There is fellowship and unity in the Godhead. Mysterious, yes, but present and beautiful. When we experience friendship or family love and unity, it is so good and blissful. And, when relationships are broken and the family is fragmented, it is so bad and painful. We long for a healthy herd.

Lately, my family and I have been the focus of herd affection, yours. The word suffocation comes to mind. I am very sensitive to that word because I am fighting to breathe everyday. Also, I know the word carries a negative image. But I am focusing on a positive, enjoyable use. Picture laughing until you are out of breath, being tickled breathlessly, or the breathlessness of a groom when his radiant bride begins her journey down the aisle. The outpouring of love we have received is astonishing—letters, cards, texts, e-mails, visits, songs, food, money, hugs, tears, prayers—the herd is suffocating me and, yet, I have never felt more alive. I feel like half of me is experiencing heaven . . . and heaven is very good.

Jesus said to the Church, His herd, *"Behold, I stand at the door and knock. If anyone hears my voice and opens the door, I will come in to him and eat with him, and he with me."*

"Come to me, all who labor and are heavy laden, and I will give you rest. Take my yoke upon you, and learn from me, for I am gentle and lowly in heart, and you will find rest for your souls. For my yoke is easy, and my burden is light."

Do you hear the tender and eager invitation in Jesus' tone? It is for you and for me. Our first fellowship must be with Him; then our other fellowships are in order. The arms of our souls must first go up, and then they can go out. This is how God's herd works.

How are our relationships doing? With God? With others? Home is best when there is peace, peace with God and peace with others.

"For to us a child is born, to us a son is given; and the government

shall be upon his shoulder, and his name shall be called Wonderful Counselor, Mighty God, Everlasting Father, Prince of Peace."

Being part of God's herd is mankind's intended home. There is peace in His house. Let's go home.

October 27, 2019
An excerpt from "Happy Birthday, Ruby Mae"

Today, October 27th, our family will be celebrating the third anniversary of the birth of our granddaughter, Ruby Mae Geiger. The Lasseter/Geiger clan will get together, play games, eat chili, cut cake, laugh and remember our little girl whose 26 days opened our hearts in ways unimaginable. It's true that we tasted the bitterness of death, but we also discovered the beauty of life–everlasting life!

Scan this QR code to hear John's song "Ruby Mae"

January 12, 2020
"Soren's Remarks at John's Memorial Service"

My name is Soren. I am John Geiger's oldest child. Many members of the Geiger family are here today, including of course my mom and two siblings. (I would never tell my brother and sister that Dad loved me the most, but, of his children, he did love me the longest, so … just connect the dots.) On behalf of his family, I thank you for being here today to remember God's work in and through his son John and to rejoice with us that death has no victory over the children of God. You are all here because you loved John Geiger, and he loved you. He might have taught your children in class, or maybe he taught you. Perhaps he was someone you looked up to as a role model and mentor. Maybe he was one of your good friends—a brother. He was a father by blood to a few of us here, but a father-figure to many, many more.

For nearly twenty years he served as headmaster of Eastwood Christian School, where he taught many classes. One of them was Rhetoric. He relished the opportunity to instruct the young on how to craft a public address and deliver it effectively. And he was pretty good at it himself. We all here have been moved by John's words. Most, perhaps all of us, have heard him deliver one of his talks on his Last Breath speaking tour. His message, delivered while looking death in the face, was powerful, even though, as the disease tightened its grip on his tongue and throat, he began to slip into what we called his J o h n W a y n e v o i c e.

I took his Rhetoric class at Eastwood, and in it he taught us that one of the key elements of an effective speech is the use of analogy to capture the attention of the audience, to develop the nuances of the topic, and to help your audience remember what you said. I have known for a long time that I wanted to speak at my father's funeral, and I knew that I needed to come up with an analogy. But I did not know which one to use … until recently, when he told me what to use.

So, many of you here have run a marathon. More power to you. Most of us here, like myself, have only seen marathons on TV, or maybe from the side of the road. All of us, though, should be familiar with the kind of runner that stands out, the one that captures the attention of the crowd. Something has set this runner apart from the rest. Maybe he's an underdog. Maybe he's overcoming great personal adversity. Maybe he is setting records at each mile marker he passes. Whoever he is, all eyes are on him. His lungs are burning as he nears the home stretch. His legs are failing him as he hits and then breaks through the proverbial wall. The salt from his sweat is caking around his mouth. He has pushed himself to the limit. People start to run alongside him, hand him water, pat him on the back, and pump their fist as he pushes forward. As the finish line comes into sight, the crowd's applause swells, and then it peaks when he crosses it.

That runner was my father during his final months and years. His body was failing him, but his spirit remained as strong as ever, it even became more determined. He was focused on the finish line and the prize that awaited him. He would not waiver from the course. And he was a crowd favorite. He captured our attention, and he inspired us. We saw him and said to ourselves, "That's how you run the race." And what else could we do but cheer him on, follow his example, and congratulate him on a race well run. Like Paul, he could say, "I have fought the good fight, I have finished the race, I have kept the faith." I shared this analogy with him two weeks ago, and he texted me, "Say that at my funeral." Yes sir.

You may also remember the story of the first marathon. It took place in the year 490 BC in Greece. The Greeks had just defeated and repelled the invading Persians at the battlefield of Marathon, so they sent one of their soldiers, Pheidippides, to run twenty-six miles all the way back to Athens in order to proclaim to the Greeks waiting anxiously there the news of victory. He ran up to the city magistrates and, with his last breath, said, "Joy, we win." The marathon my dad ran was a grueling one at the end, but that did not deter him from running hard, running straight, and running to proclaim with his last breath the joyous news that "we win." Remember 1 Corinthians 15: "But thanks be to God! He gives us the *VICTORY* through our Lord Jesus Christ. Therefore, my dear brothers and sisters, stand firm. Let nothing move you. Always give yourselves fully to the work of the Lord, because you know that your labor in the Lord is not in vain."

Let me end by encouraging you with something my father shared with me after he learned that, due to his diminished lung capacity, he only had weeks to live. I asked him if he was scared. He said, "No," but he wished his family did not have to see him suffer because he knew that what would follow would be hard. But then he reminded me that Jesus even allowed his own family and loved ones to watch him suffer and die. My father's point was not to compare himself to Jesus, but to remind me that Jesus knows our pain; he knows our hurt; he loves us through it; and he promises that one day sin and death will be no more.

So let's remember that we are all runners in this race. John just crossed the finish line before us, and he showed us how it's done. Let us run this race with perseverance. Let's stay on course. Let's encourage one another, love one another, and proclaim with every breath, even our last breath, "We win."

Selected Primary Sources

Eastwood Christian School, Montgomery, Alabama:

ECS Yearbooks, 1997-2018

Eastwood Messenger, Jun. 24, 1996; Aug. 4, 1996

Eastwood School Planning Committee Meeting agendas, Feb. 1996-Jul. 1997

Geiger Family Documents

John E. Geiger, "John Geiger—Last Breath Blog," 2018-2019

John E. Geiger, "With My Last Breath—International Tour," ca. late 2018

Steven B. Geiger, logbook, Alaska trip, Sep. 1979-Apr. 1980

Digital-Voice Recorded Interviews with Author:

Bius, Joel R., Jan. 24, 2020, Maxwell Air Force Base, Montgomery, Ala.

Gaines, Susan H., Feb. 8, 2019, Montgomery, Ala.

Geiger, Bruce R., Steven B., and Paul M., Mar. 2, 2019, Visalia, Calif.

Geiger, Dawn N. and John N. ("Nolin"), Jun. 12, 2020, Montgomery, Ala.

Geiger, John E., Aug. 10, 2018; Sep. 8, 2018, Montgomery, Ala.

Geiger, John E. and Dawn N., Jan. 19, 2019, Montgomery, Ala.

Geiger, Soren A. and Virginia (Lasseter), Jun. 29, 2020, Montgomery, Ala.

Givens, William D. ("David"), Sr., Feb. 15, 2019, Montgomery, Ala.

Jones, Cynthia W., Mar. 1, 2019, Montgomery, Ala.

Kersten, Edward L. ("Lawrence"), Sep. 26, 2019, Dallas, Tex.

Maruna, Robert E. ("Bob"), Jan. 28, 2020, Cincinnati, Ohio

Miller, R. David ("David"), Jun. 9, 2020, Montgomery, Ala.

Nolin, Andrew C., Jr., and Syble B., Apr. 13, 2019, Montgomery, Ala.

Stewart, Bruce T., Dec. 20, 2019, Montgomery, Ala.

Teal, Gregory O. ("Greg"), Feb. 21, 2020, Montgomery, Ala.

Walker, Eric M. and Mary Agnes (Geiger), Jun. 19, 2020, Montgomery, Ala.

TELEPHONE OR PERSONAL CONVERSATIONS WITH AUTHOR:

Choi, Seongho, Aug. 20, 2020

Crisler, Hannah C., May 29, 2020

Geiger, Bruce R., Mar. 3, 2019

Geiger, Gregory A. ("Greg"), Mar. 16, 2019

Geiger, John E., Jan. 5, 2019; Mar. 16, 2019; Mar. 23, 2019

Geiger, Steven B., Oct. 25, 2019

Graves, Sheila R., Apr. 23, 2020

Marion, Nathan D., May 8, 2020

McDaniel, Benjamin A. ("Allen"), Apr. 24, 2020

McDaniel, Elizabeth A. ("Beth"), May 7, 2020

McDaniel, R. Allen ("Allen") and Julie A., May 25, 2020

Powe, Erin K., Jun. 4, 2020

Pritchett, Scott P., Aug. 1, 2020

Rhodes, Amelia L. M., Jun. 1, 2020

Rhodes, Margaret D., Jun. 3, 2020

Stewart, Andrew D. ("Drew"), Jul. 6, 2020

Vaughn, Leila R., Jun. 9, 2020

Whatley, Victoria P. (Foster), May 29, 2020

E-MAIL OR TEXT COMMUNICATIONS WITH AUTHOR:

Brassell, Denise G., May 8-9, 2020

Crisler, Hannah C., Jun. 3, 2020

Draper, Glenn W., Jan. 18, 2020

Gaines, Susan H., May 26, 2020

Gamble, Samantha G., May 7, 2020

Geiger, Bruce R., Mar. 10, 2019 ; Aug. 9, 2019; Oct. 14, 2019; Nov. 24, 2019; Jun. 26, 2020

Geiger, Dawn N., Jul. 12, 2020

Geiger, Gregory A., Jun. 25, 2020

Geiger, John E., Aug. 4, 2011; Aug. 2, 2018; Aug. 31, 2018; Jan. 5, 2019; Jan. 26, 2019; Feb. 2, 2019; Feb. 23, 2019; ca. Mar. 6, 2019; Mar. 16, 2019; Mar. 28-29, 2019; Nov. 1, 2019; Nov. 15-16, 2019; Nov. 18, 2019; Nov. 23, 2019

Geiger, Steven B., Mar. 5, 2019; Oct. 14, 2019; Nov. 9, 2019; Nov. 12, 2019; Jan. 17, 2020

Grace, Lynn, Jun. 19, 2020

Hilt, Jonathan D., Jan. 18, 2020

Kersten, Edward L. ("Lawrence"), Oct. 1, 2019; Jan. 13, 2020; Feb. 25, 2020; May 25, 2020; Jun. 17, 2020

Knotts, Jerry L., Jan. 29, 2019

Lohnes, David V., Mar. 29, 2019; Jun. 30, 2020

Markwell, Ansley K., Jul. 12, 2020

McDaniel, Elizabeth A. ("Beth"), May 7, 2020

Powe, Erin K., Jun. 6, 2020; Aug. 22, 2020

Rhodes, Amelia L. M., Jun. 1, 2020 (photos); Jun. 2, 2020

Spanjer, Stephen H., Jan. 28, 2019

Sumner, Arthur L. ("Lee"), Jan. 30, 2019

Trent, Faith W. (Beaulieu), Jul. 24, 2019; Jan. 18, 2020

Walker, Mary Agnes (Geiger), Jul. 7, 2020

Wilson, Steve T., Jul. 5-6, 2020; Jul. 8, 2020

Made in the USA
Columbia, SC
02 June 2021

38865718R00117